Contents

Cover: A detail from 'Hell', a
painting by Georges Leroux showing
the inferno of Verdun
Front endpaper: A British trench
on the Somme, autumn 1916
Rear endpaper: Children taking part
in a recruiting march

Copyright © 1970: Alistair Horne
First published in 1970 by
Macdonald Unit 75
St Giles House 49 Poland St London W1
in the British Commonwealth and
American Heritage Press
551 Fifth Avenue New York NY 10017
in the United States of America
Library of Congress Catalogue
Card Number: 71-95720

Made and printed in Great Britain by
Purnell & Sons Ltd Paulton Somerset

DEATH OF A GENERATION

From Neuve Chapelle
to Verdun and the Somme

Alistair Horne

To Basil and Kathleen Liddell-Hart

Macdonald Library of the 20th Century
General Editor: John Roberts

Chapter I
The Trenches are Dug

In 1900 a Polish financier called Ivan S. Bloch made an astonishing but closely reasoned prophecy: 'Everybody will be entrenched in the next war. It will be a great war of entrenchments. The spade will be as indispensable to a soldier as his rifle.' No attention was paid to Bloch and his prophecy, because the professionals still dreamed of swift manoeuvres by bright-hued cavalry. They were still dreaming of the cavalry breakthrough in 1915 and 1916 when the trench wall — the essence and symbol of the Great War — stretched unbroken from the Channel to Switzerland.

In August 1914, the war had indeed opened with a great sweep on all fronts. While Germany was plunging her dagger into France in the West, Russia surged into East Prussia until halted at the Battle of Tannenberg. In the West, the French army in 19th-century uniforms hurled themselves towards the lost provinces of Alsace-Lorraine. German machine-guns turned the stubble fields into bright carpets of blue and red, and after appalling losses the French offensive came to a standstill. Meanwhile, the German juggernaut had rumbled — irresistibly it seemed — through Belgium and northern France, until, weakened by reserves shipped east to meet the Russian threat, it too was finally checked at the battle of the Marne.

The trench system, its significance at first utterly discounted, began to show itself north of the rivers Aisne and Vesle, where the Germans stood fast after their retreat from the Marne, in mid-September 1914. At this moment a new man in command of the German army, General Erich von Falkenhayn, saw the possibility of outflanking the Allies' left wing. The French and British countered in time, the opposing sides dug in. Then fresh outflanking movements curled out northwards, were checked, came to a halt in defensive trenches. The trench line crept insistently northwards through France with each unsuccessful outflanking thrust, in a series of man-

Left: Germans practising to fight the new war with the tactics of the old. Machine-guns soon stopped the gallant charges

oeuvres which became known (misleadingly) as the 'Race to the Sea'. The new trenches cut through the slag-heaps, brickfields, and canals of France's industrial north, and into Belgian Flanders; and south-eastwards through Champagne to the Vosges. At Ypres and Verdun two major Allied-held salients bulged into the German lines, and in 1915-16 were to give rise to some of the bloodiest fighting of the war. Nothing like these 'ramparts more than 350 miles long, ceaselessly guarded by millions of men, sustained by thousands of cannon' (Churchill) had been seen in the history of war.

The Germans, after vain attempts to break the line while it was still thin, had settled down to the defensive by the end of 1914, and they were to devote 1915 to making their trenches habitable and strong. The French and British commands, however, refused to admit the stalemate that had overtaken them. General Joseph Joffre, commanding the French army, continued small, ineffective offensive actions. Field-Marshal Sir John French, the volatile commander-in-chief of the British Expeditionary Force, soaring into sudden optimism, told his regiments in November that 'all the hard fighting was over'.

The hard fighting was indeed for the moment finished, but only because the troops were exhausted and their generals uncertain what to do. The French had lost 300,000 men killed, mostly in their initial, ill-conceived offensive, the Battle of the Frontiers, in August 1914. Britain had lost at the First Battle of Ypres in October and November an important part of her small but efficient regular army, which should have been the nucleus of her new armies to come. Germany had sacrificed much of the flower of her middle- and upper-class youth — the officers of the future — who, as student volunteers, had flung themselves recklessly into 'the massacre of the innocents' at Ypres. The Belgians who, under their clear-sighted king, Albert, had broken out so valiantly and threateningly from Antwerp and gained the Allies precious time in which to counter the final German thrust towards the Channel ports, now gathered their few, ill-equipped, poorly trained forces behind the Yser inundations, their country lost to them except for this tenuous strip.

Trench warfare crystallises
So the line of trenches was itself a line of utter exhaustion, where the contending troops had given up the hopeless battle and dug themselves in defensively. It was also a line of accident, not of planned eminences and vantage points; which made the wasteful offensives which were to follow all the more desperate, as armies launched them-

Left: The British under fire during the battle of the Marne

selves against the strongest defences for the mirage of the advantage which some ridge or hillock seemed to offer. As Churchill put it to the British Cabinet a little later, in June 1915: 'It does not seem safe to assume that particular slopes and heights possess tactical virtues of such supreme significance as to produce strategic results.'

Similarly, on the German side, the writer Rudolf Binding, an officer opposite Ypres at the end of October 1914, could see 'no strategy in this manner of conducting operations. Each of the countless divisions, like ours, is allotted a definite sector. It . . . is held to the point of senselessness . . . The war has got stuck into a gigantic siege on both sides. The whole front is one endless fortified trench'. Few were so clear-sighted.

The first, disjointed trenches were barely adequate for cover. Gradually they were linked up and made deeper, so that men could walk along them unobserved. Dug-outs were constructed. Where possible, the water was drained off; but round Ypres, and further south by the La Bassée Canal, the trenches were filled with icy water almost throughout the winter. (One British general could claim 'the men do not mind so much'. The great rift between the troops and junior officers in the trenches and the higher command safe in their châteaux, which was later to engender distrust as casualties mounted, was already discernible.) Reserve and communication trenches were started. Barbed wire was staked out in front of the lines. The opposing forces became almost invisible to each other.

Between the front-line trenches of the opposing armies ran the sinister central reserve of No Man's Land, perhaps 80 yards wide, perhaps a few hundred. Across this strip of death, the searing attacks of the next years would be launched.

The deadlock in the trenches, which was apparent by the end of 1914, had taken both sides by surprise. Everyone had expected a short war, a rapid and decisive victory. In Britain, one man, Lord Kitchener, running the War Office in field-marshal's uniform as if it were the British Army on parade, made the startling pronouncement that the war would last for three or four years, and that Britain would have to raise an army of many million men; but then Kitchener's mind operated by intuitive flashes – like a lighthouse, Lloyd George said, a penetrating beam followed by utter darkness – and the Cabinet had no very

Top left: *The first trenches begin to snake across the fields of northern France and Flanders as the opposing armies dig in. British troops prepare their lines amid the cabbages* **Bottom left:** *The finish of the race to the sea – a dead heat with neither side able to outflank the other. German troops of a machine-gun company drag their equipment over the dunes*

high opinion of his views. In the front line, fraternisation between groups of German and British troops in the fire trenches at Christmas in 1914 was still possible; and the French and Germans tended now to leave each other in peace in the quiet sectors. The unforgiving rancour of later years had not yet set in.

'Westerners' and 'Easterners'

On the German side, however, Falkenhayn had realised that it would be a long war. Following the younger Moltke's failure to reach Paris in the summer, Falkenhayn had been appointed his successor as the Kaiser's chief-of-staff, which meant in effect that he was commander-in-chief of the German army. He believed that a decision could be reached in the west, but his recognition of the strength of the Allied line on the Western Front led him to adopt a defensive policy there virtually throughout 1915. This policy, actively pursued, was to entail a constant strengthening and elaboration of the German trench system, and reliance on the withering and remorseless power of machine-gun fire across barbed wire.

The original German Schlieffen plan for the invasion of France through Belgium, so mismanaged in August 1914, had been designed to avoid a war simultaneously in the west and east, by knocking out France quickly. Now, with France undefeated and Britain at her side, Germany was faced by this very war she had feared, on two fronts. Although by mid-February 1915 the Russians had been cleared from East Prussia, Austria-Hungary was proving an uncertain ally for Germany, and was soon needing strong German reinforcements to help her hold the Russians in the Carpathians.

Germany's war in the east was being conducted by Field-Marshal Paul von Hindenburg – little more than an impressive figurehead, brought in after the first failures – with the able and decisive General Erich von Ludendorff as his chief-of-staff. Hindenburg and Ludendorff were convinced that Russia could be utterly defeated while France and Britain were held; while Falkenhayn, disagreeing, would only dole out reinforcements to the east grudgingly and too late for decisive results.

The Allies had their 'Westerners' and 'Easterners' too, though the French tended to see no further than the liberation of France's soil from the German invader. In Britain, Churchill at the Admiralty was a typical 'Easterner', looking for other theatres in which to attack the Central Powers. He toyed with landings on the Belgian coast before his logic led him farther east, to the forcing of the

Left: The stalemate and winter set in. A German sentry stands beside a makeshift shelter and peers at the distant enemy

11

Dardanelles, held by Germany's ally the Turks, and the opening up of a much-needed supply route to the Black Sea ports of Russia.

The Allied generals on the Western Front looked at their own urgent requirements in men, guns, and ammunition, and cursed the politicians for diverting supplies to other theatres. Joffre, who had lost the Battle of the Frontiers, and won, with General Joseph Galliéni's initiative and prodding, the Battle of the Marne, had already become a legendary figure as France's commander-in-chief — the embodiment of imperturbability. He believed that simultaneous offensives in different parts of the line could disrupt the German defences. He mistrusted the small British effort, carefully retained a French formation and the Belgians between the British and the sea, and felt obliged to keep galvanising the British Expeditionary Force into offensive action.

The British commander-in-chief in France, Sir John French, was a man of limited ability and unstable personality, veering sharply and immoderately from optimism to gloom, from confidence to indecision. He was over-conscious of what the French command might be thinking of him and the British Expeditionary Force, so that he was susceptible to any hint from Joffre for action by the British; although the British were not in fact in any way subordinate to the French command.

French's senior subordinate commander was General Sir Douglas Haig, commanding the British 1st Army. Haig was a different sort of man from French; he was reserved, self-disciplined, and quietly confident. He was also ambitious. He had to some extent owed the successes of his career to influence and now he started to use his friendship with King George V as a weapon against Sir John French. Already in August 1914, even before the BEF had sailed for France, Haig had told the King of his 'doubts' over the appointment of French.

Kitchener and his new armies

In France, Germany, even unwieldy Russia, war had meant mobilisation, the setting in motion of a planned machinery for bringing back into the army at once a large number of civilians who were already trained. In Britain there was only the small, highly skilled Regular Army, the bulk of which now formed the British Expeditionary Force in France. Its only potential reserve was the Territorial Army, which Kitchener mistakenly underrated and ignored. Instead, he decided to build an army of volunteers round a less reliable core, of retired regulars and of Indian army officers on leave: these were now given the immense task of forming and training what became known as the 'New Armies'. The volunteers

flocked to the recruiting offices at Kitchener's call: 'Your country needs you.' Kitchener had expected to assemble an army of 500,000 volunteers; by the end of 1914 he had nearly 1,000,000, and the machinery for training and equipping them creaked badly.

At the front, the British regulars were sceptical. Kitchener's 'ridiculous and preposterous army of twenty-five corps is the laughing stock of every soldier in Europe', declared one senior general, '. . . under no circumstances could these mobs take the field for two years'. The generals expected, anyway, to have broken through the German lines long before then.

The winter of 1914-15 in fact gave the Allied commanders no grounds for this optimism. The invincible sweep of machine-gun fire across No Man's Land was already demonstrating its defensive power, and the enemy's barbed wire entanglements, covered too by machine-guns, were proving a murderous barrier in front of his better-sited trenches.

The wire became the new horror. It 'terrified and obsessed the infantryman. All his daring and courage came to naught when he ran against an incompletely destroyed network. He knew that he would get caught and lacerated in its entangled mass of snares and meshes. His would be a slow, agonising death'. The German wire had to be destroyed if any attack was to succeed, and high-explosive shells were the weapon. But these were in desperately short supply. Starting with more in the first place, the Germans had been quicker than the Allies to expand their own supplies of artillery and ammunition. The French, having concentrated on their light 75s designed for offensive action in open country, were seriously short of heavy guns capable of oblique fire; but the British lack of guns and shells was far more critical. The firepower of the British artillery was quite inadequate even for the defence of its own trenches, let alone for the pulverisation of the enemy's wire. In the factories in Britain, Kitchener's recruiting for the army had resulted in a grave shortage of skilled munition workers, which in turn led to a disastrous shell shortage.

Lacking artillery support, lacking the weapons of trench warfare, the mortar and the hand-grenades, dependent on their own rifle fire to contend with patrols and local attacks, short of trained junior officers and NCOs, the British infantry had to man their trenches in strength, unable to rely on their guns to ease the burden of defence.

Left: 'The men do not mind so much' claimed one of their commanders. British troops trying to find a way to drain their trench discover the reality and discomfort of the trenches

Patterns of warfare

The pattern of trench warfare, which was to eat up the years, was now emerging. The German defence, with strong, permanent trenches guarded by the almost unbreakable partnership of barbed wire and machine-guns, was building itself a fortified barrier of enormous strength. The Allied generals, with an optimism which was to prove quite unfounded, believed that they could break through with well-prepared offensive actions, supported by a concentration of artillery fire-power which they did not yet possess. Joffre, and his subordinate General Ferdinand Foch, now in command of the French armies in the north of France, though temperamentally different, were united in their amazing optimism, and in their plans for early offensive action and for tying in the British with their schemes. They flattered French and they shamed him; they allowed it to be known how little the French army thought of the BEF as a weapon of attack after its winter failures.

A closer and even more disturbing presence to French was that of Haig, coolly critical and supremely sure of his own calm judgement and ability. Haig saw the immediate obstacle clearly, the lack of guns and shells, but thought too readily that artillery would utterly destroy the German defences: his dream of the final cavalry manoeuvre — his own arm — blinded him perhaps to the infantryman's tactical problems. Although some of Haig's instructions in 1914 and early 1915 show that he was aware of the problem of the machine-gun, he was also capable of pronouncing at this time that it was 'a much overrated weapon'. Like most other commanders, French and British, he underestimated the strength of the German positions, summing the matter up for *The Times* correspondent in January 1915: '. . . as soon as we were supplied with ample artillery ammunition of high explosive, I thought we could walk through the German lines at several places.'

So the stage was set for the five offensives the British and French were to make against the German lines in 1915 — each of them planned to be the great breakthrough. The men themselves — as well as the generals — were keen; the French to redeem their sacred soil, the British to have another go at the Hun as a change from the wretched winter, crowded in their inadequate, halfflooded trenches.

Left: As both sides dug in and fortified their lines, the long queues of men going forward and casualties going back began to stretch behind them. German troops in a French town

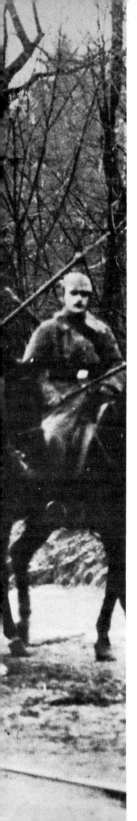

Chapter II
1915 — The Spring

Joffre at the beginning of 1915 was planning to make 'two big efforts to break through the German front' as soon as the ground was dry enough. One attack would be made in Artois by the French 10th Army, to the north of Arras against the Vimy Ridge, and by the British on their left. The other attack would be made simultaneously by the French in Champagne, where he expected to achieve more. Joffre made it a condition of the 10th Army attack that the British would first relieve the French 9th Corps, which was holding the line to the north of the British 2nd Army at Ypres. But Sir John French would not and could not both relieve the French corps and launch an offensive, especially since his reinforcement problem was now aggravated by preparations at home for the attack on the Dardanelles.

Both French and Joffre stood obstinately firm, and the 10th Army attack on Vimy Ridge was thereupon cancelled. This left Sir John in a dilemma: he wanted badly to redeem the good name of the British Expeditionary Force, and to appear to be helping Joffre; but merely to relieve a French corps in the trenches north of Ypres would not make much of a showing. He therefore resolved that the British should attack alone, and not wait even for Joffre's grand Champagne offensive — which in the end never came to anything.

French has been blamed for the recklessness of this decision. But the morale of his troops was low after their winter in the trenches, and he considered that action, and of the British army's own seeking, would do much to put fresh heart into them.

Haig had his 1st Army sights fixed on the Aubers Ridge, opposite his northern sector — a low feature in the flat industrial countryside; but beyond it lay the city of Lille, which the Germans had made the HQ of Crown Prince Rupprecht of Bavaria's VI Army in Artois. This front was at that time lightly held; the Germans, like Joffre, had formed a poor opinion of the British after the winter's failures.

Left: German Hussars patrol behind the lines in Belgium

Keep on sending me

OXO

From one of the
British Expeditionary Force

"When I returned to my
billet very cold & wet, your
parcel was lying on my blanket.
You can guess the first thing
I did was to make a cup of
OXO, and I and my
chums declared on the spot
this cup of OXO was
the best drink we had
ever tasted."

Haig had therefore been planning an attack against the slight German salient round the village of Neuve Chapelle. French gave him the go-ahead on 19th February. Haig was especially anxious to achieve surprise, and had decided to concentrate the fire from the considerable artillery he had been given – 372 guns – in a short, shattering concentration of 35 minutes, against a sector of only 2,000 yards, immediately before the infantry attacked. Surprise was a factor which Haig was to ignore in later battles. Before Neuve Chapelle, the shortage of artillery ammunition may have been father to the thought, demanding in itself a short bombardment.

The aeroplane, though still rather a patchwork of fabric and wire, was beginning to play its part in reconnaissance at the beginning of 1915. The Royal Flying Corps had photographed the whole of the German position at Neuve Chapelle, and so it was possible to provide the army with large-scale maps showing the Germans' trench network in detail. There had been an accurate estimate, too, by British Intelligence of the small German strength in front of them – on the sector where the opening blow was to fall with about 40,000 men, there were in fact barely 1,400 Germans.

Success seemed assured, and Haig brushed aside a suggestion that the narrowness of the front (which, like the shortness of the bombardment, was in the beginning dictated by the lack of shells) might prove a bottle-neck for the large number of troops in the attack. At 7.30 on the morning of 10th March, the British guns opened up their devastating fire against a defence line which was a simple breastwork built up on the water-logged soil, and only lightly wired.

The British attack at Neuve Chapelle

When the fire lifted from the German line to Neuve Chapelle village at 8.05, the infantry of 4th Corps on the left and of the Indian Corps on the right quickly crossed No Man's Land, to find the first enemy line shattered, the support line empty, and the surviving German troops surrendering or running away. After three-quarters of an hour they had captured Neuve Chapelle itself; after an hour-and-a-half they had reached their objective for the day. Ahead of them the fields were empty.

*Far left: Two versions – for home consumption – of life in the trenches. A joking German postcard **(top)** showing jolly musketeers with a signpost pointing to the 'rifle range' and notices saying 'Furnished room to let' and 'Villa of German tranquillity'. A British poster **(bottom)** extolling the virtues of 'Oxo'. Left: The contrast, men of the Cameronian regiment trying to brew their Oxo in a front-line trench in the winter*

19

Dunkirk

may 1915

Aubers

apr 1915

Ypres

Neuve Chapelle
Lys R.

mar 1915

Béthune

Armentières

Loos

La Bassée

sep 1915

Arras

Vimy

Lille

Douai

Somme R.

Amiens

Bapaume

Cambrai

Pozières

Albert

Flers

Péronne

Oise R.

Compiègne

Soissons

Meuse R.

Rheims

French offensive
December 1914
February - September
1915

Vauquois

| 20 | 40 | MILES |
| 20 | 40 | 60 KM |

Verdun

Western Front 1915

Losses on the Western Front 1915

1915

France
1,624,000

Great Britain
296,583

Germany
873,248

Yet it was not until after 11 am that orders reached them from the rear, and these were that 'no further advance was practicable'. Thus, through excessive caution and inadequate communication, the opportunity to exploit a clear break into the German line was utterly lost. The flanks of the British attack had not been successfully safeguarded and the two corps commanders, not fully realising the degree of their success, were unwilling to risk a further advance.

It was now that the British staff-work broke down, partly through the insufficiency of communications—a pattern that was to be repeated on the Somme the following year. The attacking troops were halted beyond Neuve Chapelle; but the large body of reserves was still pushing up behind them and filling the narrow gap of the break-through, so that 10,000 men were standing about and waiting in the mud for their corps commanders to integrate their text-book moves. It was fortunate that the German artillery in this sector was still so weak.

As Charteris, Haig's Intelligence officer, put it, 'the whole machine clogged and stopped'. But Haig himself did not intervene at first, and the advance was not set in motion again till the Germans, having been given five clear hours, had assembled enough reinforcements to check the British infantry, which, converging into the bottle-neck, but still under the commands of two separate corps, were quickly confused and disorganised when they came under fire.

On the second day the British made no progress, their losses rose, and the Germans improved their defences.

The Germans were no more masters of the offensive in this new trench warfare than the British. At dawn on the third day they launched a counterattack with sixteen battalions, but spread out along the whole Neuve Chapelle front, so that it was easily repulsed and their losses were heavy. The British, however, again failed to follow up this advantage, and in the afternoon Haig felt impelled to urge the two corps to push forward 'through the barrage of fire regardless of loss'; and loss was all that they achieved. Only next morning did he issue orders to the front units to consolidate their positions. In all, they had gained a dent, 1,000 yards deep and a mile and a quarter wide.

Neuve Chapelle was important because it set a pattern for the Allied offensives which were to follow—frontal attacks after bombardment, whatever the state of the

Far left: The Western Front in 1915 showing the five main Allied offensives—each of which was meant to be the final breakthrough—and the German attack in which gas was first used. Left: German troops outside their billet behind the lines

defences, regardless of loss. The real lessons – the value of surprise, and a rapid, well-organised follow-up of any successes – became submerged. The German, Binding, was already able to write after Ypres in 1914: 'As matters stand now, not only here but all along the line, both we and the enemy have so crippled ourselves by in-fighting that we cannot get in a blow properly, we cannot get the momentum for a thrust; we get in our own way with every movement of any importance.' These words could equally be describing the failure at Neuve Chapelle.

First Gas Attack at Ypres

While the Allies were digesting the lessons of Neuve Chapelle, the Germans attacked at Ypres; not with any really serious intent, but experimentally, for Falkenhayn was already engrossed in the Eastern Front, where Germany and Austria-Hungary were about to embark on an overwhelming spring offensive against the Russians. So he was unwilling and unready to commit himself to any major offensive on the Western Front.

In the late afternoon of 22nd April 1915 the Germans, simultaneously with an intense bombardment of the town of Ypres itself and villages in the Allied rear, released chlorine gas from cylinders in two clouds, on either side of the village of Langemarck, against the French troops holding the northern sector of the Ypres salient. The French troops there were not of the highest quality, and they had had no warning of the possibility of gas; so very soon those who had not been asphyxiated at once were seen fleeing back in droves towards Ypres and the canal, vomiting, pointing to their throats, calling out 'gaz, gaz'. In no time they had left a gap in the line 4 miles wide, empty of any soldiers except the dead and those still dying in agony.

The British, so far unaffected, saw it all with amazement: '. . . more curious than anything else was a low cloud of yellow-grey smoke or vapour, and, underlying everything, a dull confused murmuring.

'Suddenly down the road from the Yser Canal came a galloping team of horses, the riders goading on their mounts in a frenzied way; then another and another, till the road became a seething mass with a pall of dust.

'Plainly something terrible was happening. What was it? Officers, and staff officers too, stood gazing at the scene, awestruck and dumbfounded; for in the northerly breeze there came a pungent nauseating smell that tickled the throat and made our eyes smart. The horses and men were still pouring down the road, two or three on a horse, I saw, while over the fields streamed mobs of infantry, the dusky warriors of French Africa; away went their rifles, equipment, even their tunics that they might run

22

the faster. One man came stumbling through our lines. An officer of ours held him up with levelled revolver. "What's the matter, you bloody lot of cowards?" says he. The Zouave was frothing at the mouth, his eyes started from their sockets, and he fell writhing at the officer's feet...'

The Germans pushed forward in pursuit across the empty French trenches in considerable strength. The Belgians on the canal, at the hinge with the French, had escaped the worst of the gas, and gave only a little ground, though attacked with full force.

In the French sector, the Germans advanced 2 miles that evening, unopposed, and then stopped, though only scattered parties of French, Canadian, and British troops, hastily improvised, stood between them and Ypres itself. But the Germans, though attacking in strength, had only one division in reserve behind them; and now the troops were starting to walk into their own gas.

The German failure to follow up the devastating element of surprise afforded by the first use of gas squandered the great advantage that might have been reaped from the cruel 'secret weapon'. (In 1945, Hiroshima *did* stop a war.) The British would repeat the same error with tanks in 1916. Once the surprise of gas had been sprung, thereafter the Allies were always in a position to retaliate with gas more effectively by reason of the prevailing westerly winds.

The German use of gas should not in fact have been the complete surprise it was. German prisoners had been bringing in evidence since the end of March. But the French ignored it, and the British, after a half-hearted air reconnaissance, were content to forget it all. No hint was passed down to the troops.

The Germans themselves had been issued only with the crudest form of respirator, and were glad to limit their advance and start digging in across the middle of the French half of the salient. On subsequent days too, when Ypres still lay virtually open to them, they were content to advance step by step, wherever they were certain that gas or their powerful artillery had cleared the ground.

Fighting at Ypres continues
The British sector of the Ypres salient—the southern sector—was left isolated by the French collapse. The Canadian Division was attacked with gas early on 24th April. Their only protection against the gas was handker-

Left: Zouaves with the first primitive gas masks. They were the first troops to be attacked by this new secret weapon

chiefs, towels, or cotton bandoliers wetted with urine: they resisted magnificently, but were eventually pushed back. Binding came forward with the Germans: 'All the dead lie on their backs, their fists clenched; the whole battlefield is yellow.'

Ypres never fell. Its ruins were saved by the desperate efforts of the British and Canadians. Again and again Sir John French, who was intervening personally in the battle, ordered them into hopeless counterattacks across the open ground, whose slight rises were now held by the Germans. 'When dawn broke in our battered support trench it was evident enough that we were all in the hollow of a great bowl, with the Germans sitting on the rim and shooting at us.' The casualties were appalling. By the evening of 25th April the Canadians had lost 5,000 men.

Foch, who was co-ordinating the Allied effort at Ypres, promised glorious French counterattacks, which the British would support. But his own corps commander, Putz, would not budge; and the British attacks continued, alone, in a vain cause. Smith-Dorrien, commanding the 2nd Army, recommended a withdrawal from the narrow, exposed half-salient to a flattened line covering Ypres and the canal. French had him sent home. Plumer, who succeeded, was allowed to undertake this very withdrawal a few days later, during the first three nights of May. 'No one,' wrote an officer of the Lancashire Fusiliers, 'for a moment felt that, in resigning the ridiculous triangle of battered ground to the Germans, we were retreating or giving away anything to his advantage . . .'

But even this smaller British salient round Ypres remained 'one huge artillery target', and the battle continued until the Germans started running short of shells in the last week of May. Of over 100,000 casualties on both sides during this Second Battle of Ypres, more than half were, for once, among the defenders; for the British and Canadians had lost 60,000 men. The results at Ypres were to give Falkenhayn thoughts about the other Allied salient at Verdun the following year.

Meanwhile, British and 'Anzac' troops, with some French units, were fighting another costly losing battle on the Dardanelles. They had landed on the Gallipoli peninsula on 25th April (the fourth day of Ypres), and their failure was terrible.

On the main Eastern Front, on 2nd May, Mackensen's XI Army and the Austro-Hungarian IV Army started attacking across the Carpathians as the spearhead of a massive offensive to sweep the Russians out of the Austro-Hungarian province of Galicia. By the end of May, the Russian strength in this sector seemed broken. Italy

entered the war on the Allied side on 23rd May; but Falkenhayn persuaded the Austrians to remain on the defensive against Italy, and not withdraw troops from the Russian front.

Joffre attacks in Artois

While the fate of Ypres still hung in the balance, Joffre launched his long-delayed offensive in Artois on 9th May, with the British attacking simultaneously some way to the north—once more, in physical isolation, on either side of Neuve Chapelle. The French attacked north of Arras, towards the Vimy Ridge, under Foch's direction, with nine divisions of d'Urbal's 10th Army in the forward line and another nine in reserve. A new French discovery, 59-year-old Philippe Pétain, was commanding 33rd Corps in the centre, opposite Souchez, on a 4-mile front. His preparations for the attack were meticulous, and his corps broke through the Bavarian-held lines to advance 2 miles, almost to the crest of Vimy Ridge. But French reserves were slow in coming forward, and too few.

The French had come up against German defences of unparalleled strength and complexity, a system of trenches and fortified villages, dominated by three concrete redoubts, equipped with underground shelters. These had survived five days of preliminary bombardment, and were ready to receive the attackers with well-organised machine-gun fire. The Germans had learnt well the lesson of Neuve Chapelle in March.

By the night of 12th May, Pétain's 33rd Corps had gained the commanding height of Notre Dame de Lorette. But on either side the French attack had been halted or thrown back with terrible losses, so that Pétain's troops were stranded well forward on much too narrow a front, their communications destroyed by shell-fire. The Germans, regrouped in this sector under General von Lochow, now managed to establish a new defence line to hold Pétain, though Foch persisted in further vain attacks.

The French had failed to learn, on their side, three of the lessons of Neuve Chapelle: the need for the attacker to have reserves immediately ready to exploit any success; the dangers of an exposed salient if it cannot be widened out; and the difficulties of communication between front and rear under heavy and persistent artillery fire. Pétain's success was at first ignored, because 29 ▷

Top left: A British recruiting poster urges volunteers to come forward to replace the men lost at Neuve Chapelle. For the first time the British, with their massive frontal attacks, were experiencing the terrible casualties which were to become such a feature of their offensives on the Western Front. *Bottom left:* A German convoy takes reinforcements to the front. *Next page:* A romantic view of the Canadian defence of Ypres

telephone lines had been relied on and had been cut; and this meant too that the French artillery continued to shell ground which French troops had won.

The French attacks flared up again for a few days in the middle of June: Joffre felt it his duty to make a show of further aid to the hard-pressed Russians. When the offensive was finally abandoned, the French had lost 102,500 men, the Germans only half that number.

Haig, attacking to the north, met with a day of unrelieved carnage and failure on 9th May. The bombardment was inaccurate, with a high proportion of dud shells, filled, according to the Germans, with sawdust and manufactured in America. The British infantry surged out in strict lines, dressing by the left, as they had been trained, and were mown down by the enemy's machine-guns. A German war diary describes the attack: '. . . there could never before in war have been a more perfect target than this solid wall of khaki men, British and Indian side by side.' At midday Haig came forward to put pressure on the corps HQs. He was given an estimate of casualties, and 'took it very hard. We had been getting reports all morning of how well the French were doing and he must have felt that they would be laughing at our efforts, as they did in December'. Next morning Haig's three corps commanders were able to persuade him not to pursue the offensive, using the very real shortage of ammunition as their excuse.

On this one day the British had lost 458 officers and 11,161 men, and had achieved nothing. When they attacked a few days later at Festubert, spurred on by Joffre, results were little better.

The Allies had won themselves no real advantage in these spring offensives of 1915, only very heavy losses in manpower. Joffre would always console himself that, even where no advance was gained, the German losses were significant too. It was all part of his strategy of 'nibbling' at the enemy, as he put it. But attrition was not at present favouring the French and British. Russia had not been helped: the failure of these assaults, in fact, encouraged Falkenhayn to pursue the campaign in the east more vigorously, and allow the Western Front to look after itself. Moreover, the shells and manpower put into the western offensives could well have tipped the balance in Gallipoli, though British leadership failed there too. For all this sacrifice, as Churchill pointed out, of approximately 19,500 square miles of France and Belgium in German hands, the Allies had recovered about eight.

Left: Two French grenadiers wearing the new gas masks. **Next page:** *'A battery being shelled' by Wyndham Lewis. An artist's impression of the horrors and savagery of the new mass warfare*

29

Chapter III
1915—The Autumn

The continued German and Austrian successes on the Eastern Front during the summer of 1915 did a lot to divert attention in Germany from the losses that had been suffered in the west: by the middle of August the Russians had been pushed back across Poland to the line of the upper Bug, as much as 200 miles from the German starting line of 2nd May.

In France, Joffre, with so little to show in Artois for the shattering casualties, was under heavy criticism. President Poincaré, for one, was left with 'no illusion whatever as to the Arras operations, which have utterly failed'. When he visited the Arras front in July, a corps commander asked him to do what he could 'to put a stop to these local offensives. The instrument of victory is being broken in our hands'. Joffre, however, weathered the storm and continued to plan for the next offensive, for a breakthrough in the autumn.

Fearing for his own position after his spring disasters, Sir John French launched a political counteroffensive at home in the middle of May, using the military correspondent of *The Times,* Colonel Repington, who happened to be visiting the front just then, as his weapon. He provided Repington with true, if somewhat slanted evidence, much of it secret, on the British shortage of artillery ammunition. The uproar which these despatches provoked, since they flatly contradicted many of the government's reassurances, strengthened the Conservative opposition's case for demanding the reshaping of Asquith's government to atone for the Dardanelles; and a coalition government was formed on 19th May.

This press campaign led to the creation of a Ministry of Munitions under Lloyd George. But it did French himself no good. Behind his back, the King and Haig agreed that it was 'all most unsoldier-like'; and Kitchener too was arranging private channels of communication with Haig. It would not take much now to pull the carpet from under French's feet.

Left: Exhausted British troops are led from the line after the battle of Loos. They went forward in high spirits but were swiftly shattered by machine-guns, artillery, and barbed wire

Co-ordination of strategy between the Allies had not so far been carried to any high pitch. As far as the Western Front went, it had depended largely on the persuasive powers of Joffre and Foch and the loyalty to them of French and Haig. Now, early in July 1915, leading members of the French and British Cabinets met to formulate a strategic plan for the rest of 1915. Kitchener, also present, seems to have fallen under Joffre's spell, for by the middle of August he was giving Joffre's plans for a big attack his full support. Yet Kitchener's light had gleamed again in July, when he had noted: 'The French have an almost unlimited supply of ammunition and fourteen divisions in reserve, so if they cannot get through we may take it as proved that the lines cannot be forced.'

Joffre's plan for the autumn offensive was more grandiose than ever, and his optimism was supreme. His aim was to pinch out the great German bulge round Noyon, which remained an uncomfortable threat to Paris, by a Franco-British attack eastwards in the coalfields of Artois, towards Lens, and a simultaneous French attack far away in the chalk downs of Champagne, northwards, halfway between the French-held cities of Rheims and Verdun. These attacks were to be followed by a general offensive which would 'compel the Germans to retreat beyond the Meuse and possibly end the war'. In each case, cavalry divisions were kept champing and snorting in immediate reserve, ready to exploit the breakthrough — which, as usual, would never come.

French attack in Champagne

In Champagne, in the bare hills between the Suippe and the upper Aisne, the French, with the attack fixed for 25th September, started active preparations on 12th August. A great network of support lines and communication trenches — leading forward to the fire-trench at every 300 or 400 yards — was dug to a depth of 3 miles, and new roads were built across the barren countryside. Despite every effort at camouflage and deception, the German III Army opposite, under General von Einem, quickly became aware of what was going on, since the workings in the white chalk showed up everywhere, and air reconnaissance revealed many new branch railways being built behind the trenches.

The French intended attacking on a 15-mile front with two armies — one now commanded by Pétain. In overall command was General de Castelnau, the recently appointed commander of the Central Group of Armies.

Everything, it seemed, had been thought of by the French staff, and the failures of previous offensives would be avoided. Telephone lines were doubled and trebled, and reserves placed in close support. The artillery in par-

ticular was in enormous strength: they amounted in all to 900 heavy guns, which bombarded the German lines for 75 hours before the infantry attacked. Surprise, of course, was utterly lost, but this seemed to the French command of little importance when they could dispose of such unparalleled might.

The French infantry, cushioned by this show of strength and resolve, and proud of their newly-issued steel helmets and horizon-blue uniforms, were in good spirits. Their initial attack, supported by gas and smoke, was highly successful: the three-day artillery barrage had thoroughly churned up the German front trenches, the enemy dead lay everywhere, prisoners streamed in, and there were only small pockets of resistance, though German artillery fire was sometimes uncomfortably heavy. The first wave of the French infantry swept forward irresistibly: '. . . our artillery, leaving the emplacements where they had been anchored a whole year, came across and took up position in the open, a magnificent spectacle. Squadrons of cavalry came up. Suddenly the long, sombre trench warfare was at an end.'

It was not. The Germans had learnt their lesson too from the precarious situation the French had put them in north of Arras in May. Here, in Champagne, beyond the ridge, 2 to 4 miles behind their front line, they had dug a second defence line, even more strongly manned than the first line of trenches. This second line took the French completely by surprise. The Germans let them come right up to the wire, which the French artillery had not yet touched, before letting loose a hail of fire. The French troops in the second wave were then caught out in the open by the German guns, which were directed onto them by aeroplanes and observation balloons.

In their initial success, the French had advanced up to a mile and three-quarters and had taken 18,000 prisoners, and the Germans were badly shaken. But nowhere could the French break into the second German line. Bad weather prevented their artillery from destroying it, and on 28th September the French were forced to break off the offensive. The Germans had successfully initiated defence in depth, and the French were beaten by it.

Artois and Loos

The French Artois offensive of 25th September, planned as the grand complementary thrust, turned out to be another prod in the direction of Vimy Ridge. The French missed Pétain's determination this time, but had the British attacking simultaneously on their left flank at Loos. Here, as in Champagne, bad weather limited the artil-

Left: Joffre watches his troops going forward to the trenches

35

lery's accuracy, and the French had too few heavy guns to destroy the enemy's defence positions thoroughly. Their 75s, their staple guns, barely touched the concrete of the German emplacements. There were still deadly machine-guns left which, even in isolation, could mow down the French as they came across the open ground – always, of course, in perfect formation. A French officer described how 'Three hundred men of our regiment lay there in perfect formation. At the first whistling of bullets, the officers had shouted, "Dress by the left!" and they all went to their death as on parade.'

Sir John French had been very much averse to attacking at Loos, across a bleak coalfield, with cover given to the enemy by pit-heads and mining villages: he would much rather have made the British offensive at Ypres. But within a fortnight his schoolboy loyalty to Joffre had overcome his reservations, and he had agreed that Haig's 1st Army would attack towards Loos and Hulluch. At first French tried to get away with making it an artillery offensive and withholding the infantry, but Joffre quickly found him out and put on pressure for a full-scale British attack.

British and French co-ordination, at any level, still left much to be desired. In planning the attack, Sir John remarked to his commanders 'that it was easier to gain information about the strength and composition of the enemy's forces than about the French'. And Robert Graves, on being introduced as a junior officer to the front line that spring, had been told: '. . . there's never any connexion between the two armies, unless a battle is on, and then we generally let each other down.'

The British were attacking with six divisions against one German division. They were planning, like the French, to use gas, and because of their shortage of high-explosive shells and heavy guns (117 in all) they were having to put much more faith in the disruptive effect of the gas. The situation at dawn on 25th September was therefore very tense at Haig's HQ, when it appeared doubtful whether there would be enough wind to carry the gas, emitted from cylinders, across to the German lines. Haig wrote in his diary: 'At one time, owing to the calm, I feared the gas might simply hang about *our* trenches. However, at 5.15 am I said "carry on" . . . But what a risk I must run of gas blowing back upon our own dense masses of troops!'

These tailored sentiments, this high decision, contrast with Graves's trench view of this moment in history: 'It seems that at half-past four an R.E. (Royal Engineer) captain commanding the gas-company in the front line

Left: British troops on parade in the first rudimentary gas masks

phoned through to divisional headquarters: "Dead calm. Impossible discharge accessory [code-word for the gas]." The answer he got was: "Accessory to be discharged at all costs." . . . the gas went whistling out, formed a thick cloud a few yards off in No Man's Land, and then gradually spread back into our trenches. The Germans, who had been expecting gas, immediately put on their gas-helmets: semi-rigid ones, better than ours. Bundles of oily cotton-waste were strewn along the German parapet and set alight as a barrier to the gas. Then their batteries opened on our lines. The confusion in the front trench must have been horrible; direct hits broke several of the gas-cylinders, the trench filled with gas, the gas-company stampeded.'

Where the gas carried well, the initial British attack achieved some success: the cost, however, was extremely high, largely through the ineffectiveness of the artillery in destroying the German wire and neutralising machine-gun emplacements. On this front, as in Champagne, the Germans had been preparing a second line of defence, covering La Bassée in the north and Lens in the south (as the British had been disturbed to discover in July); and it was fire from this line which finally pinned down and broke up Highland troops of the 15th Division who had fought their way over the summit of Hill 70, one of the attack's objectives.

On their right flank, troops of the 47th Territorial Division had taken Loos. As the London Irish approached the village, 'There was no haste in the forward move, every step was taken with regimental precision, and twice on the way across the Irish boys halted for a moment to correct their alignment.'

A little further north, a mixed force from the British 1st Division broke through the German second line at Hulluch, and were opposed by only scattered forces. But troops who could have reinforced and exploited this important British breakthrough were thrown away elsewhere and decimated on futile frontal assaults. By the evening the British had been forced back out of the Germans' second line. Yet for the thinly-spread Germans the situation earlier in the day had been serious, and HQ staffs and orderlies had had to join in the defence.

Sir John French, meanwhile, had stationed himself near Lillers, 25 miles away from his own chief-of-staff, without even a telephone. What is more, he had insisted on keeping the reserve corps under his own hand; partly out of unwillingness to throw two of its divisions, the 21st and 24th, which were among the first from Kitchener's New Armies, and only recently arrived in France, straight into battle; and partly, it seems, out of jealousy of Haig. If Haig had had these reserves ready under his

command, in close support, the incipient break-in at Hulluch, though very narrow, could have been exploited.

In the end, the two New Army divisions, despite their total inexperience, were thrown into the battle, but not till the second day, 26th September. Because they had been held too far back, they arrived after a long and confused night march, without proper food, and had to attack under conditions which by then had swung back heavily in the enemy's favour. The Germans had been given the chance overnight to reinforce and strengthen their second line; whereas the two British divisions were attacking in the full light of mid-morning, without any appreciable artillery preparation or support, and with no possibility of surprise. So they advanced in their dense ranks across open country, swept by artillery and machine-gun fire.

The spirit of these New Army volunteers was very high: 'they were delighted at the prospect of getting at the enemy'. Their courage as they advanced against the wall of machine-gun fire and rifle fire was incredible. But the German wire broke them.

The German XV Reserve Regiment, brought up to reinforce their second line at Hulluch, faced the 24th Division's attack. The regiment's diary describes it: 'Ten ranks of extended line could clearly be distinguished, each one estimated at more than a thousand men, and offering such a target as had never been seen before, or even thought possible. Never had the machine-gunners such straightforward work to do nor done it so effectively. They traversed to and fro along the enemy's ranks unceasingly. The men stood on the fire-steps, some even on the parapets, and fired exultantly into the mass of men advancing across the open grass-land.'

The two British divisions had attacked with a strength of just under 10,000. In three and a half hours they lost 385 officers and 7,861 men. The Germans had virtually no casualties.

The British command classed Loos, like Neuve Chapelle, as a victory. But 'Victory was to be bought so dear,' wrote Churchill of the 1915 battles, 'as to be almost indistinguishable from defeat.' If, in these autumn offensives, the Allies claimed that they had at least bought experience, this was even more true of the Germans, who were also readier to profit by their lessons.

Left: Throughout the autumn of 1915 the Germans remained on the defensive, content to fight off the Allied attacks from well-prepared lines of fortification. A German soldier mounts a fire-step to throw grenades while repulsing an Allied attack

Chapter IV
Year Without a Dawn

The year 1915, with its fruitless and costly offensives, has been well named '*l'année stérile*'. The optimistic or non-committal communiqués, the cheery front-line propagandists, could not hide, from those at home all over France or in Britain, the passage and arrival of the train-loads of wounded, nor silence the persistent talk of mismanagement they brought with them. Yet Ian Hay allows one of his characters, returning from leave in London in the late summer of 1915, to say: 'People seemed quite surprised when I told them things out here are as right as rain.'

In France the generals again survived the mounting criticism. They could always speak of the territory of eternal France regained from the enemy, even if it were only to be measured in square yards. Joffre was even promoted, to be overall commander-in-chief of the French army in all theatres.

It was the French government which suffered from the failed hopes of the autumn offensive. Viviani, who had headed the first all-party government since the beginning of the war, was replaced by the liberal Briand; and Galliéni, the saviour of Paris in 1914, became War Minister. The Chamber of Deputies was now demanding a greater say, with secret sessions, examination of generals, visits to the front, and a more exact control over the running of the war.

In Britain it was the army's turn, and Sir John French was made its scapegoat. His own chief-of-staff, Robertson, now joined Haig in intriguing against French with the King, who, in those far-off days of princes, still had, as titular head of the army, considerable influence. Haig was provoked into becoming more open in his criticism of French by their violent disagreement over the availability of the reserves at the battle of Loos. Whatever justification French may have had for not allowing them to be committed at once, he blundered after the battle

Left: The Kaiser and the Crown Prince visit German forces in France. During 1916 Germany turned away from the east to concentrate on defeating France and Great Britain in the west

by trying to cover up, with wrong dates and times in his despatches, the delay in handing the reserves over to the 1st Army. Haig would have none of this. By the middle of December 1915 it was settled. French was given a title and posted to the home front; Haig got his job as commander-in-chief of the British forces in France; Robertson was made Chief of the Imperial General Staff.

Haig and Robertson kept these appointments for the rest of the war. They trusted each other, and they proved an unbreakable combination. They both believed firmly in the overriding importance of the Western Front: victory, to them, could only be won there, and the sole tactics they knew of involved frontal assault on the German lines with a prodigious expenditure of shells and men. As France progressively weakened after Verdun, and Britain with her new armies became the stronger member in the alliance, so the partnership of Haig and Robertson was to set the course of the whole war. Lloyd George and other doubters, who saw the waste and futility of the Western Front, had little power against them.

Kitchener's star had waned, like Churchill's a few months earlier, with the progressive failure of the Dardanelles campaign. Now, at the end of 1915, there was nothing left but to wind up that expedition, and the Cabinet had sent him out to make the final decision.

On other battlefields
In October 1915, war had flared up in the Balkans, where Germany and Austria-Hungary had decided to deal finall with Serbia and open up communications with their ally Turkey. For this, the Central Powers made an alliance with Bulgaria, who was able to attack Serbia in the flank while the Germans and Austrians pressed in from the north. The Allies sent a predominantly French force to Salonika in neutral Greece in order to help Serbia from the south, but there was little they could do to help the defeated Serbs. The Allies were foolishly to maintain and even increase their force in Salonika, to no immediate purpose; so that half a million valuable French and British soldiers were kept locked up in what the Germans dubbed 'the greatest internment camp'.

By September 1915 the Russians had been driven out of Poland to a line from the Gulf of Riga to the tip of Roumania. Their resistance seemed broken, they had lost over 750,000 in prisoners alone and territory bigger than France; but they were still able to build a defence line.

Far left: General Falkenhayn. His plan for an all-out German offensive centred on the Verdun salient forestalled the new French offensives being planned by Joffre (left). Commander of all French forces, Joffre chose to disregard warnings of the impending German attack and refused to strengthen Verdun

Falkenhayn, seeing his triumphant armies moving off eastwards away from their railheads and supplies, had exercised caution, and had prevented Ludendorff from carrying out an ambitious encirclement at Vilna until it was too late. Now Falkenhayn had lost the chance of destroying the Russian army, and had thereby given Ludendorff the key he wanted for his own eventual overthrow.

With Serbia settled and Russia apparently no longer a danger, Falkenhayn was glad to close his ears to the nagging of Hindenburg and Ludendorff and start making plans for an all-out offensive in the west in 1916: it was there, he considered, that the decision must lie. His Austrian ally Conrad, in turning away from the east for similar reasons, looked not west but south, where the Italians had been attacking viciously but ineffectively along the Isonzo river on their north-eastern frontier with Austria-Hungary, hoping to gain Trieste. Conrad felt it was now time to finish with Italy. So he and Falkenhayn, each bent on his own moment of decision, turned their back on one another at the close of the year.

Allied plans for 1916
In contrast, the Allied camp was at last attempting to draw closer together and co-ordinate its strategy, instead of relying on the mere moral persuasiveness of fatherfigure Joffre. A conference was held on 6th December, at Chantilly, Joffre's headquarters of the commanders of the French, British, Belgian, and Italian armies, with representatives from Russia and Japan. This conference was more military and more formal than the Anglo-French meeting of July, though the decision it reached was hardly one to raise eyebrows: there would be a simultaneous general offensive in 1916 by France, Britain, Russia, and Italy. More important was the discussion on the timing of the offensive. It was realised that Russia needed to re-equip. Britain's shortcomings in manpower and ammunition, too, were recognised with greater patience than hitherto, and it was agreed to wait until the summer, when the Russians would be stronger, the British New Armies would have had more adequate training and front-line experience, and there would be an abundance of heavy guns and shells. Joffre spoke of the 'brilliant tactical results' of Champagne and Artois in the autumn; and their experts fooled them with figures showing that Germany was running out of reserves.

Joffre and Haig, the latter now the British C-in-C, met again at the end of December to discuss the Western Front's contribution to the big offensive, and on 14th February they agreed that it should be a joint attack astride the River Somme.

In July 1915 there had been twenty-one British divisions in France; at the end of 1915 there were thirty-six, and two Canadian. The New Armies which Kitchener had raised were beginning to make their contribution. On the other hand, the Indians had been unable to stand the Flanders climate: the Indian Corps had been disbanded and the troops sent to the Near East.

The French had at this time 105 divisions in the west, the Belgians six; the Germans had, out of their 159, 113 divisions on the Western Front, facing the Allied total of 150. The French, despite their apparent numbers, were running into a man-power crisis, having already drawn on their capital by calling up the younger classes a year early during 1915. 'The French are now looking to England and Italy to carry on a wearing out attack until they and the Russians are ready,' Haig confided to his diary in January 1916. He saw the coming shift in the balance of power between the Allies: 'I think that the French man-power situation is serious as they are not likely to stand another winter's war. There is no doubt to my mind but that the war must be won by the Forces of the British Empire.'

There was now less deference to the French. Haig, unlike his predecessor Sir John, was to stand firm in opposing Joffre's scheme for preliminary 'wearing-out' attacks; but he did agree to the Somme, when he would have preferred to make the main British offensive in Flanders.

The British army was now bigger than anything Britain had put in the field before, and it was beset with all the problems of organisation and command which its size, sudden growth, and inadequate training brought with them. But it was still not nearly big enough, and in January 1916 the historic step of introducing conscription in Britain was made.

British man-power problems over the manufacture of munitions were also being ironed out by Lloyd George. The shortage of artillery ammunition in Britain's 1915 battles had been very real. French had made an estimate of his ammunition requirements in December 1914, before the scale and intensity of the Western Front offensives could be envisaged. By May 1915, only something like one fifth of this estimate was being supplied to the BEF. British commanders in the field, therefore, as they correctly insisted, had not been supplied with the weapons for the job; but this very admission only increases their share of blame in 1915, for their unjustifiable optimism, and for repeatedly hurling their infantry against defences which could not, by objective calculation, have been destroyed by bombardment.

Left: Kitchener (centre), father of the New Armies, visits the front

45

Nor, as Churchill saw in June 1915, were shells the whole answer: 'It is remarkable that during eight months of trench warfare, ingenuity seems to have had so little success in discovering means of offence and advance. We are now somewhat readily accepting the proposition that high-explosive shells used in unprecedented and extraordinary quantities will achieve decisive results. This has certainly not been proved by the results so far attained by the French offensive.'

Weapons and relative casualties
At least the French had attacked with the assurance of having better supplies of ammunition and of heavy artillery. In Champagne they had had two and a half times as many heavy guns to the mile as the British at Loos. But both the Allies were short of heavy, high-trajectory guns throughout 1915. The new French 105-mm gun and the short-barrelled quick-firing 155-mm were yet to appear in any quantity.

From the earliest days of 1915, the Germans had been well supplied with trench-mortars, with which they did much damage. Such luxuries were in extremely short supply in the British trenches, and the troops of both Allies suffered from inadequate hand-grenades: the French in their 1915 autumn campaign were still equipped with grenades which went off in their hands; and on the British side the new Mills bomb was only trickling in. Graves describes the summer of 1915, 'early days of trench warfare, the days of the jam-tin bomb and the gas-pipe trench-mortar: still innocent of Lewis or Stokes guns, steel helmets, telescopic rifle-sights, gas-shells, pill-boxes, tanks, well-organised trench-raids or any of the later refinements of trench warfare'. The French were generally having to make do with too flimsy a machine-gun, the Saint-Etienne: it was only gradually being replaced by the stronger Hotchkiss. On the other side of the line, it was the German strength in front-line armament, as well as their comparatively ample supplies of artillery shells, which enabled them not only to defend themselves so superbly when attacked, but also to relax in their concrete shelters when not under attack, even in some comfort, with only a minimum guard, or to take cover during bombardment.

It was factors such as these, as well as the German defensive policy in the west and the prodigality of the Allied attacks, that had made the German casualties here so much lower than those of the French and British. In the autumn offensives, the British casualties were

Left: A recruiting parade in London. In spite of heavy losses Britain did not impose conscription until the start of 1916

47

60,392; the Germans opposite them lost barely 20,000. The French casualties in Champagne and Artois in the autumn were 191,797; the Germans opposite them lost 120,000 — a more balanced ratio. In general terms, the Allies had lost 250,000 men in the autumn to the German 150,000. These losses were heavier than any side could really stand. France had by now lost half her regular officers. Britain's regular army was a mere skeleton. Germany's smaller losses must be set in the framework of her smaller man-power in the west: in Champagne she had opposed, including reserves, thirty-five French divisions with sixteen; in Artois, seventeen French divisions with nine; round Loos, twelve British divisions with five. German strength had lain in their organisation of defence, in concrete, wire, and machine-guns. The Allied weakness had lain not in man-power but in equipment, in the strategy of frontal assaults and their imperfect coordination, and in the unimaginative handling of troops in the attack.

The writer of the British Official History remarks that 'the year 1915 is not one on which the nation and the Army can look back with satisfaction'; and that in the western theatre 'the enemy undoubtedly had the best of the fighting'. Binding wrote in the German lines in Flanders: 'Enthusiasm is dying bit by bit. It is losing its resilience like a spring that has been compressed too long in the same position. That is what distinguishes this war — on all fronts, in every theatre of war, the feeling of insufficiency. No one has strength enough.' 'The year closes,' wrote President Poincaré on 31st December 1915, 'without any ray of the dawn of victory.'

Yet Germany and the Allies were both preparing to attack on the Western Front in 1916 with the greatest confidence. 'On all sides,' writes Cyril Falls, 'there was stark determination to achieve victory at all costs. So numerous were the combatants, so heavily had they been armed by the growth of warlike industry, that, whether or not the deadlock was broken, the losses and all the miseries of war were certain to increase. In fact it proved to be a year of killing.'

Bottom right: Sir John French and the men who engineered his dismissal at the end of 1915 — General Sir William Robertson (top right) his chief-of-staff who became Chief of the Imperial General Staff, and General Sir Douglas Haig (right) who became commander of the British forces in France — a position which he was to hold — against all opposition — until the end of the war

Chapter V
The Watershed—1916

1916 was to be the year of Verdun and the Somme, the great and tragic watershed of the war. Beyond it all rivers run in changed directions. It was the year that saw German hopes of outright victory vanish, and the Allied prospects of winning the war with their existing tactics and resources—without the United States—disappear. It was the last year in which Russia would be a powerful military force, and by the end of it Great Britain would have assumed the principal burden on the Western Front.

On both sides, armament was to reach a colossal peak and the large numbers of big guns would provoke the commanders in the field, firm in their belief that artillery could destroy defence, to these two gargantuan battles.

The troops of 1916 were the best the war had produced. In the German army and the French, the hard core of regulars, who had borne the brunt and the losses of the early battles, were now leavened with reservists and conscripts, experienced in battle too. The scrapings of the French manpower barrel had not yet reached the front line; and on the German side, those weighed down by the long, wearisome months of defence were now buoyed up by the presence of comrades from the Eastern Front, fresh from their exhilarating victories over the Russians. The British, in turn, were keyed up by the rapid expansion of their army and the prospects of power and victory which it brought. The New Armies, flooding now into the front lines, were made up of Kitchener's volunteers—'the flower', as Alan Clark puts it, 'of the richest, most powerful, nation on earth'.

More conscious, perhaps, than anyone of the growing strength of Britain was the German commander, Falkenhayn. Shortly before Christmas 1915 he presented a long memorandum to the Kaiser. He saw Britain as 'the arch-enemy of this war'. Except with unrestricted submarine warfare, which the German navy ought to pursue to the limit in 1916, there was no way Germany could strike directly at Britain. The only course was to knock out of her hand Britain's 'best sword'—the French army.

Left: *The Crown Prince reviews German troops near Verdun*

51

To break the French army, Falkenhayn considered that 'the uncertain method of a mass breakthrough, in any case beyond our means, is unnecessary. We can probably do enough for our purposes with limited resources. Within our reach behind the French sector of the Western Front there are objectives for the retention of which the French General Staff would be compelled to throw in every man they have. If they do so, the forces of France will bleed to death . . .' Principal among these objectives was the fortress city of Verdun.

So a new concept was added to war. Never before had any great warlord proposed to vanquish an enemy by gradually bleeding him to death. The macabreness of its imagery could only have emerged from that Great War where, in their callousness, leaders could regard human lives as mere corpuscles.

Falkenhayn, reserved, hard-working, and ruthless, was one of the most able commanders of the war on either side. He must be given the credit for bringing Germany safely, even triumphantly, from the disasters of the Marne in 1914 to the arrogant peak of the Verdun plan. There was, however, a recurrent element of indecision in him. This had lost the Central Powers the chance of crushing Russia out of the war in 1915. Now, in his plans for Verdun, Falkenhayn was prudently avoiding the attempt at a mass breakthrough; but with his cautious, step-by-step onslaught he was to lose control of its momentum, and bleed white not only the French army but also his own.

The successful (but not decisive) outcome of the 1915 campaign against Russia had enabled the Germans to move nearly 500,000 men from the Eastern Front to the Western, and Falkenhayn felt himself at last rid of the restriction of fighting a war on two fronts.

As it happened, and perhaps through intentional flattery on Falkenhayn's part, Verdun came within the command of the Kaiser's heir. An intelligent, musical, pleasure-loving, and pathetically inexperienced general, the Crown Prince ('Little Willie') had as chief-of-staff of his V Army a paragon of Prussian military efficiency and resolution, General Schmidt von Knobelsdorf. By mid-December 1915, Falkenhayn had won over the Kaiser, and he and Knobelsdorf were already planning the details of the attack on Verdun.

From the very start, Knobelsdorf's own plan of attack was based on an approach to Verdun not only from the north and north-east, but also from the north-west, up the left (western) bank of the Meuse; to take full advantage of the existing German noose round the Verdun salient by attacking on all three sides. Such a total commitment was quite contrary to Falkenhayn's

conception of the gradual, 'bleeding-white' attack: he wanted to attack on the right bank of the Meuse only. This would be threat enough to Verdun to draw in the French; anyway, he maintained adamantly that the Germans did not have the numbers for a left-bank attack.

Knobelsdorf was right: this decision of Falkenhayn's not to get round behind Verdun at once from the north-west frustrated the whole operation. The Crown Prince agreed with Knobelsdorf, but saw no use in pressing the matter further. Falkenhayn then left all preparations in the hands of the Crown Prince and Knobelsdorf, but kept a strict watch that they did not overstep the initial limit in men and materials he had set.

Fortress Verdun

Verdun was an ancient fortress and had been considered throughout French history as a vital gateway into central France. It had become the most imposing of Vauban's chain of fortresses in Louis XIV's reign, and had been the last of the great French fortresses to fall to the Germans in 1870. After 1871 it became the key bastion in the chain of fortresses guarding France's diminished frontiers, when the Germans had annexed Alsace and Lorraine. In 1914 it had acted as the eastern pivot of the French line and had made Joffre's recovery on the Marne possible. Falkenhayn had correctly appreciated that Verdun had an almost sacred value, which the French would feel bound to defend to their last gasp.

The Meuse flows northwards through Verdun, cutting its path in great loops and deep gorges through a plateau, which itself is broken up by hills and ridges, some of them steep, but nowhere rising more than 1,000 feet or so. In 1916 they were often heavily wooded. For the French they formed strong natural defence lines. Their commanding heights were studded with three concentric rings of underground forts, 4 miles or more out from Verdun itself, intended as an outer defence against the approach of an enemy's artillery. The outer forts had been strengthened with concrete and steel, and some of the major forts were equipped with retractable steel turrets.

What these Verdun forts lacked now, however, was guns. The fall of the strong Belgian forts at Liège and Namur in 1914 had come as a shock to the French command. The Germans had been able to wreak great damage on them with their new weapon, the enormous 420-mm mortars, the 'Big Berthas', the biggest guns used in the war. In August 1915, therefore, Joffre was able to persuade the government to allow the Verdun forts to be dismantled and their valuable artillery – the equivalent

Left: The Duke of Brunswick wishes the assault troops luck

53

of forty-three heavy batteries and eleven field-gun batteries — transferred to the field, where they added their great weight to the neighbouring offensive in Champagne in September and October. When the guns had gone, the men too were pushed out of the forts into the open, where they dug themselves inadequate trenches, aware that in the discarded forts at their back they had a safe bolt-hole. So the all-round defence provided by the Verdun forts was poorly replaced by a single trench position.

The Verdun salient had been quiet for so long that the troops there were infected with a chronic lethargy, which the commanding general, Herr, an elderly gunner, was unable to dissipate. The barbed wire was incomplete, there were no underground telephone lines, no shell-proof shelters except the forts, no communication trenches. In Pétain's words: 'Between the forts and beyond them there was nothing but dilapidation: countless trenches which had largely fallen in, jagged ends of wire . . . tracks and roads reduced to quagmires; equipment scattered about, the wood rotting and the metal rusting.'

Against this moribund sector of the French defence line the Germans now set the whole power of their military organisation. Ten new railway lines leading up to the V Army's front were built, train-loads of equipment were carried in. Entire villages were emptied of their inhabitants to make room for the 140,000 soldiers assembling for the attack. But the main weight of the German effort was concentrated on their artillery.

On the north side, the German lines were less than 10 air miles down the winding Meuse valley from Verdun itself. The French defences round Verdun and the citadel itself provided an excellent artillery target. What the Germans hoped to save in manpower in the attack they would spend prodigally in high-explosive shells. Their heavy guns would blast so deep a hole in the French lines that the infantry might follow through with only slight casualties; and their artillery barrages would grind to pieces the successive reinforcements which the French were expected then to send into the salient.

By day and night the German guns flowed in along the newly built railways, many of them from the Eastern Front and the Balkans. There were thirteen of the 420-mm (17-inch) Big Bertha mortars. (Contrary to popular belief, the super long-range gun that shelled Paris in 1918 was not called 'Big Bertha'. The true 'Big Berthas' — named after the Krupp heiress — were short-barrelled mortars with only limited range.) There were seventeen of the Austrian 305-mm mortars; these and the

Right: *German troops move a 210-mm howitzer into position*

54

Big Berthas were to concentrate on the Verdun forts. There were two long-barrelled, long-range 380-mm (15-inch) naval guns, one of which was to drop forty shells a day on Verdun itself, the other to interrupt communications on the west bank of the Meuse. The quick-firing, easily transportable 210-mm guns were intended to pulverise the French front line, and then to prevent reinforcement coming up: there was a battery to every 150 yards of trench. The long-barrelled 150-mm guns would be eliminating any new French guns that might appear and raking all roads and tracks leading up to the front: 'no line is to remain unbombarded, no possibilities of supply unmolested, nowhere should the enemy feel himself safe.' Finally, there was the new weapon of horror, the flame-thrower, which made its debut at Verdun.

By 1st February all the 1,220 guns were in position to support an assault front of barely 8 miles.

Overwhelming secrecy

An overriding consideration was secrecy – a lesson the Germans had learnt from the Allied mistakes of 1915. No visitors were allowed, and preparations were ostentatiously pursued for a 'deception' attack on Belfort. Even Germany's ally Austria-Hungary was tactlessly kept out of the picture. The most important innovation was the construction of great concrete underground galleries, in which the assault troops would assemble before the attack, instead of visibly cramming the front-line or jumping-off trenches and inviting premature artillery fire, as the Allies had so often done.

To help guard this secrecy, the aeroplane now came fully into its own. The Germans had sprung a march on the Allies with the introduction of the Fokker monoplane in October 1915. It had a synchronising gear, which ensured that the bullets from its machine-gun passed between the blades of its propeller. The Fokker, fast and manoeuvrable, was to remain superior to all other types until May 1916, when the French brought out the Nieuport Scout. At the beginning of 1916 the Germans used their current air supremacy above all to ward off any French attempts to send their aircraft scouting over the lines and taking back evidence of the immense German preparations. For the first time the Germans were thus employing their aircraft massed defensively, as fighters, and trying to create a kind of aerial barrage through which French aircraft would be unable to penetrate. Some French aircraft, of course, did get through, but their reports were not sufficient to cause any ripple in the complacent calm which pervaded French GHQ.

Joffre was now as ostrich-like over Intelligence reports of German intentions as he had been earlier over the state

56

2ᵉ **EMPRUNT**

DE

ÉFENSE NATIONALE

Souscrivez

NET

ritte

GS-

IHE

of the Verdun defences. The previous governor of Verdun had been sacked for disagreeing with Joffre's disarming of the forts; and now Herr, quite unable through shortage of men and materials to carry out the many tasks set on him, was merely ignored. 'Everything had been started, and nothing finished': there was not even a second line of trenches. It was a French deputy, Driant, serving as a lieutenant-colonel in command of two battalions of *Chasseurs* in the north-eastern extremity of the salient, who managed to get reports through to the Defence Minister, Galliéni, on the poor state of the Verdun defences. Joffre rebutted his charges. Joffre's Operations branch regarded the absence of German jumping-off trenches opposite Verdun as conclusive evidence that no attack was being planned. Admittedly, the Germans' extensive deception plans and feints were having their effect, but Joffre and his staff had convinced themselves that the Germans were not going to attack in the west in 1916, and they were entirely taken up with the initial plans for the Allied offensive on the Somme in the summer. There, where their armies joined, the French and British would attack together on a broad front, 'arm in arm', the French with forty divisions, the British with twenty-five. The objective in this sector was perhaps not clear, but the comradely effort on a front of nearly 40 miles would bring success, and the cavalry would go through.

This dream-world in Joffre's Operations branch, however, was being ever more insistently disturbed by the nervousness at Verdun. Joffre's chief-of-staff, de Castelnau, paid a visit there late in January, followed by President Poincaré. Eventually even Joffre himself turned up, and, still more to the point, a reinforcement of two divisions, which were handed over to Herr on 12th February – the day originally intended for the opening of the German offensive.

The Intelligence branch at French General Headquarters, in contrast to Operations, was now quite convinced of an impending assault on Verdun; and 'most of the staff at General Headquarters were excited at the idea of the coming struggle and kept their eyes fixed on both banks of the Meuse,' wrote one of Joffre's officers. The sceptics in the Operations branch continued to toil away at their dispositions on the Somme for the coming summer, the abundance of heavy guns, the Kitchener New Armies. But on 21st February, 'the bear blew first'.

Left: The strain of more than eighteen months of war begins to tell on the resources of the contestants. French (top) and German (bottom) posters make appeals for war loan subscriptions

Chapter VI
Verdun

When day dawned on 12th February 1916, the day fixed for the assault on the Verdun salient by the Crown Prince's V Army, the ground was already covered with deep snow, a blizzard still raged, and mist lay over the whole landscape, blanketing the artillery's targets. The opening German bombardment was therefore postponed.

So tardily had Joffre woken up to the dangerous situation opposite Verdun that the coming of the blizzard on this very night saved the defences from being overrun at once. The two newly-arrived French divisions were not yet in position on 12th February. If the Germans had attacked on this day with their seventy-two battalions of chosen assault troops, they would have found the French defenders in half-completed positions, caught in the midst of moving house.

It can be argued that, strategically, the immediate loss of Verdun would not have been such a bad thing for the French. The fortress had been dismantled, and the French line would have been shorter and stronger without it. But the French nation would hardly have stood the shock of such a withdrawal. Falkenhayn thought not; and Briand, the French Prime Minister, felt certain that his government would not survive it.

For nine days the weather played its part in the defence of France, with snow, fog, rain, and gales. The troops on both sides waited tensely. The Germans probably suffered more, keyed up as they were for the attack. Their concrete galleries were not intended as a permanent shelter for large numbers of troops; so most of them had to walk to and from distant billets through snow and freezing sleet. In this weather, too, the galleries filled with water, and pumps were in short supply. Baling icy water on nine days of emergency rations was hardly the way to keep shock troops in fighting condition.

The German attacking force, from the Meuse at Consenvoye eastwards, comprised three corps, or six divisions: VII Reserve Corps under von Zwehl; next, on a short sector

Left: 'Hell' by Georges Leroux, a French artist's impression of the inferno which surrounded Verdun at the height of the battle

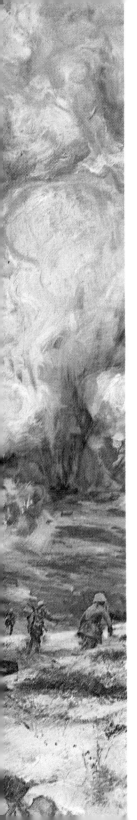

opposite the Bois des Caures, XVIII Corps under von Schenck; on their left, III (Brandenburg) Corps under von Lochow. By 21st February there were still only three French divisions – Chrétien's 30th Corps – facing the Germans.

The bombardment begins

The weather improved on 19th and 20th February, and at dawn on the 21st the German bombardment started in all its planned intensity. For nine hours the appalling bombardment continued. It was a concentration of high-explosive shells, a sheer weight of metal, which the Western Front, despite the great artillery barrages of 1915, had never known before. From front to rear in the narrow sector of the impending German attack, nothing was spared. The French trenches, poorly prepared, were obliterated and many of the troops manning them were buried. To the 72nd Division detachment of *Chasseurs* under Lieutenant-Colonel Driant in the Bois des Caures, opposite the German XVIII Corps, it seemed as if the wood were being swept by 'a storm, a hurricane, a tempest growing ever stronger, where it was raining nothing but paving stones.' And apart from the din of the explosions there was the splintering crash as the great oaks and beeches were split or uprooted.

About mid-day there was a sudden pause, and the French troops emerged ready to face the German infantry. But it was a trick; the bombardment started again, with new concentrations by the short-range heavy mortars, but the same implacable fury.

Even when the bombardment finished in the afternoon, the Germans were taking no risks. Instead of the long, dense, vulnerable lines of an Allied attack, their infantry came forward on this first day as powerful fighting patrols, making skilful use of the ground, probing for the sectors of least resistance; and wherever they used the new flame-throwers they caused panic in the French ranks. But they would enlarge the gaps only on the next day when the main weight of the attack went in. Zwehl alone had the initiative to expand his orders, and followed up his patrols immediately that afternoon with the first wave of storm-troops, who managed to effect the initial breach of the French defences.

This first day had not gone as well for the Germans as they had expected. The concentration of shell-fire was meant to destroy all life in the French front-line defences; but the blanket had not been consistent **65** ▷

*Left: Another of the new weapons, German troops using a flame-thrower. **Next page:** 'A gigantic luminous serpent which never stopped and never ended', a painting of 'La Voie Sacrée', the single tenuous lifeline leading to Verdun, by Georges Scott*

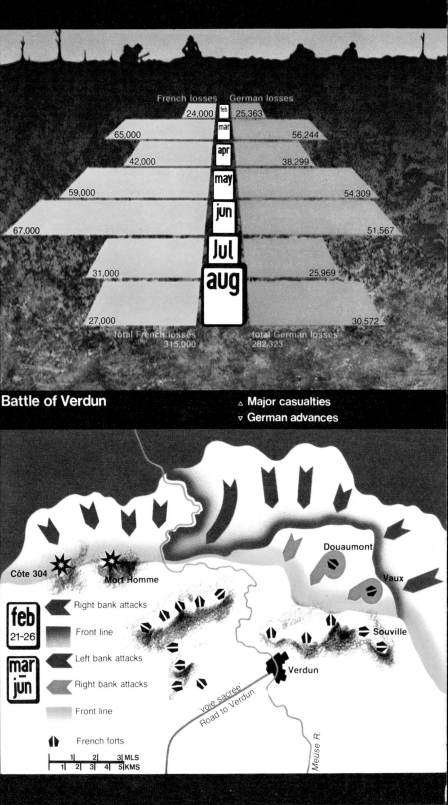

French losses   German losses

24,000	feb	25,363
65,000	mar	56,244
42,000	apr	38,299
59,000	may	54,309
67,000	jun	51,567
31,000	Jul	25,969
27,000	aug	30,572

total French losses
315,000

total German losses
282,323

Battle of Verdun

△ Major casualties
▽ German advances

Douaumont

Côte 304

Mort Homme

Vaux

feb
21-26

▸ Right bank attacks

▪ Front line

**mar
-jun**

▸ Left bank attacks

▪ Right bank attacks

▪ Front line

Souville

Verdun

'voie sacrée'
Road to Verdun

♦ French forts

| 1| 2| 3| MLS
| 1| 2| 3| 4| 5|KMS

Meuse R.

enough, there remained stubborn and heroic pockets of resistance, and the German infantry were disturbed to meet such dangerous opposition.

Next morning, 22nd February, the bombardment began again. With great dash, several French units attempted counterattacks, but their means were too small. However, it took XVIII Corps all day to clear Driant's *Chasseurs* out of the Bois des Caures, so spirited and flexible was the defence. The French artillery, too, had improved their shooting and were reinforced. Flanking fire from French batteries on the left bank of the Meuse was starting to cause trouble: the weakness in artillery of the German VI Reserve Corps on the left bank, an economy of Falkenhayn's, was now a distinct disadvantage.

That afternoon German flame-throwers crushed the last resistance in the Bois des Caures, and Driant was killed. But the German losses had been unexpectedly heavy, their confidence was shaken, and their offensive had been held up during one whole day—a day vital to the French command—by Driant's resistance in the very centre of the attack. Now the French field-guns were being silenced one by one by the fire of the long-barrelled 150s.

On 23rd February the Germans made surprisingly little progress, even though the French continued to suffer enormously. On a rise behind the Bois des Caures, in the true style of the Western Front, infantry of the German XVIII Corps pressed forward in dense formations, wave after wave, to be scythed down in turn by the French machine-guns. Official German records speak of this as a 'day of horror'.

By that evening, the 72nd and 51st divisions, with an original combined establishment of 26,523, had together lost 16,224 officers and men. The Germans, on the other hand, despite their rebuffs, felt that Verdun was now theirs for the taking.

Breakthrough

So it was. The whole French second position, inadequately prepared to start with, and now pounded out of existence, was overrun on 24th February in three hours.

The French 37th African Division—the dreaded Zouaves and Moroccan *Tirailleurs*—had been brought up to fill the gap left by the 72nd Division. Cowed by the bitter, freezing weather, beaten down by the incessant bombardment, and split up into small units under strange officers, some of the North Africans lost their nerve and fled. By the night of 24th February, French morale was crumbling

*Far left: The Verdun salient showing the main German attacks and the French defensive positions. **Left** from the top: The rival commanders: Falkenhayn, Knobelsdorf, Joffre, and Pétain*

seriously. Their artillery was silent, their clearing stations overflowing with untended wounded, their wounds often frozen by the intense cold. Only a fraction could be got out: the German 380s, firing with 'diabolical precision', had cut the only full-gauge railway out of Verdun. Chrétien's 30th Corps was finished. The vanguard of Balfourier's 20th Corps, which was to relieve them, had arrived from the Lorraine front, cold, hungry, and exhausted, and was thrown into the battle at once.

That evening of the 24th, de Langle de Cary (the commander of Army Group Centre) obtained permission from Joffre to shorten the line and withdraw from the Woëvre Plain to the Meuse Heights east and south-east of the city. Later that night, with the news worse, Joffre, against all precedent and orders, was rudely wakened after his bed-time by de Castelnau. Aroused at last, Joffre despatched de Castelnau at once to Verdun with full powers to do whatever was needed. De Castelnau arrived at breakfast-time on 25th February, found Herr 'depressed' and 'a little tired', went straight to the battle-torn right bank, and effected miracles in reanimating the defence: 'Wherever he went, decision and order followed him'. He estimated that Verdun could be saved, that an effective defence could be maintained on the remaining cross ridges. He informed Joffre by telephone, gave orders that the right bank of the Meuse should be held at all costs; and he called in Pétain, considered to be a master of the defensive, to command the Verdun salient. So the terrible decision was taken to defend Verdun to the limit – as Falkenhayn had banked on in his December memorandum.

On the morning of 25th February, except for continued French resistance in front of VII Reserve Corps, the Germans had before them only the powerful forts ringing Verdun. Fort Douaumont was the first that lay in their path, and the strongest. From every angle, its great tortoise hump stood out, imposing, menacing, fascinating. It was, in fact, only occupied by a small detachment of territorial gunners, who were manning the 155-mm turret gun which had survived Joffre's purge, and its approaches were inadequately covered. In one of the most remarkable feats of the war, small detachments of Brandenburgers managed to edge into the fort unobserved during the afternoon of the 25th and to capture its elderly occupants, without losing a single man.

The effect of the fall of Fort Douaumont was electric. In Germany church bells rang. In Verdun itself an officer ran through the streets crying 'Sauve qui peut!', and civilians poured out of the city, jamming the vital roads. The remnants of the 37th African Division made a needless and dangerous withdrawal.

Pétain takes over

Pétain took over command at midnight. The mere knowledge that he was in command stiffened the French resistance and gave new heart to the troops, so high was his reputation already. The arrival at the same time of the main body of Balfourier's seasoned 20th Corps, the 'Iron Corps', marked the turning point. All troops in the salient were now regrouped under four corps commanders within Pétain's 2nd Army, and fresh reserves were beginning to pour in.

Pétain realised that the loss of Fort Douaumont did not mean final disaster, that the other forts could be manned and linked into a formidable defence perimeter. He issued orders accordingly: from this line there must be no withdrawal. At the same time he had the artillery reorganised into one concentrated and effective weapon. From this moment, says the German official history, 'began the flanking fire on the ravines and roads north of Douaumont that was to cause us such severe casualties'.

It was the precarious supply route into Verdun which concerned Pétain next. The railway had been rendered useless by the German long-range shelling. The only substitute was motor transport on the one road in, the second-class road from Bar-le-Duc. Lorries were requisitioned, gangs of territorials detailed to devote themselves entirely to the upkeep of the road, and the highway itself was strictly reserved for the ceaseless flow of motor traffic in both directions. Any lorry that broke down was heaved aside into the ditch. At night, the procession of dimly lit vehicles resembled 'the folds of some gigantic and luminous serpent which never stopped and never ended'. It is astonishing that the Germans never thought of bombing the road, which could so easily have been blocked. Eventually, vehicles were passing for hours on end at a rate of one every five seconds: the equivalent of more than a division of soldiers was kept mending the road. It was the artery through which the life-blood of France flowed into Verdun. Maurice Barrès gave it the immortal name of *La Voie Sacrée*.

The Germans bog down

By 28th February the German attack on Verdun was virtually brought to a standstill. The French were fresher and more determined, their original divisions replaced and then reinforced, whereas the German formations had not been relieved at all and their troops were feeling the strain of a week's intensive fighting: promised

Left: 'You eat, you drink, you sleep in the midst of dying, you laugh and sing in the company of corpses'. The defenders of Verdun crouch amid the ruins during a brief lull in the battle

67

reserves were not forthcoming. The German artillery was flagging under the extreme difficulties of moving forward over the violently cratered ground, especially when a thaw turned the clay to deep mud. Worst of all, the French had increased their heavy guns in the salient from 164 to more than 500, and they were shelling the German infantry with continuous and effective flanking fire from the left bank of the Meuse, in particular from the forts on the Bois Bourrus ridge.

Pressure within the Crown Prince's V Army was therefore intensified for the opening of an attack on the left bank of the Meuse, especially with a view to capturing the commanding height of the Mort Homme. As late as 26th February, with the right bank apparently within the Germans' grasp, Falkenhayn had again refused permission for an attack on the left bank; but the next few days changed his mind, and he gave his consent on 29th February, at the same time sending up the reinforcements that he had previously withheld.

By then the moment was passed. The German reserves now committed – quite apart from those held uselessly opposite the currently inoffensive British front in the north – would have ensured a German breakthrough on the right bank to Verdun itself on 25th or 26th February. The wish to economise the German forces and to draw the French into the right bank fighting had achieved the effect of drawing the Germans themselves in on terms that were not their own: the battle itself was starting to take control.

Meanwhile, the German losses continued to mount. Their wounded streaming back were 'like a vision in Hell'. Franz Marc, the painter, wrote in a letter from the Verdun front on 3rd March: 'For days I have seen nothing but the most terrible things that can be painted from a human mind.' He was killed next day by a French shell.

At this time, the French were gradually wresting back air superiority over the battlefield. Some sixty of the top French air aces – those heroes of single combat like Brocard, Nungesser, Navarre, and Guynemer – were banded together into the famous *Groupe des Cigognes* (the Storks). Altogether the French brought in 120 aeroplanes over Verdun, to set against the Germans' 168 aircraft, fourteen observation balloons, and four Zeppelins. Poor German tactics and French verve tipped the balance, and in the next two months, while the German balloons were shot down in flames, French ob-

Right: By day and night the transports moved up La Voie Sacrée to keep Verdun fighting – the road was never cut by the Germans even though it was the only supply route to the city

servation planes were to contribute greatly to the success of their artillery. The German aces, Boelcke and Immelmann, failed to upset the French supremacy, which the new Nieuport fighter later helped to consolidate.

The Mort Homme

When the new attack came, on 6th March, starting with a bombardment comparable to that of 21st February, the Germans at first had considerable success. They took the Meuse villages of Forges and Regnéville and advanced towards the bare ridge of the Mort Homme on its north-eastern flank. The French 67th Division gave ground too readily following the bombardment, and over 3,000 of its men surrendered. But a brilliant bayonet charge at dawn on 8th March held the Germans and forced them to delay the final assault on the Mort Homme. The front on this north-eastern approach barely shifted for the next month.

On 14th March the frontal assault on the Mort Homme began. German reserves were flowing more freely now, and it seemed there was no limit to the men and shells they were willing to expend to gain possession of this desolate hill. A deadly pattern was established that continued on this sector for the next two months. After hours of bombardment, the German assault troops would surge forward to carry what remained of the French front line, which was no longer trenches but clusters of shell-holes where isolated groups of men lived and slept and died. When the German attack had exhausted itself, ground down by the barrages from the French guns on the Bois Bourrus ridge to the south-east and on Côte 304 to the west, the French would counterattack within twenty-four hours and drive the surviving Germans back again. But each flow and ebb of the tide brought the German high water mark a little further forward. The cost was terrible: by the end of March, 81,607 Germans had been lost and 89,000 French, with a high proportion of senior commanders as casualties in this compressed battle area.

On the bare slopes of the Mort Homme, the Germans lost their tactical advantage. There were no woods or ravines here to favour infiltration; their flame-throwers, now that the pioneers who wielded them were targets in open country, had become suicide weapons; and the French flanking fire was here even more crippling. In attempting to eradicate the French artillery on their flank, the Germans had merely brought on themselves a new source of flanking fire, from the neighbouring hill, Côte 304, to the west of the Mort Homme. So this too would have to be attacked and taken.

The capture of a key position at the base of Côte 304

on 20th March gave the Germans no further advantage, only staggering losses under the French machine-gun fire. Signs of exhaustion and unwillingness to attack were increasing amongst them. Their divisions were being kept too long in the line, and the gaps in their ranks filled with unseasoned youths. Pétain faced the same problem by insisting, through his *Noria* system, on a rapid rotation of units: no division remained more than a few days under fire. As a result, two-thirds of the French army were to be fed through the 'mincing machine' of Verdun, and its reserves drained.

On 9th April a simultaneous attack was mounted on Côte 304 and the Mort Homme. Only a secondary crest of the Mort Homme was reached; and on Côte 304 the French guns continued firing on the exposed German flank.

The summit of the Mort Homme now became a long-drawn battle of desperation as the contestants swayed backwards and forwards between the two crests, and the artillery of both sides turned the hill into a smoking volcano. 'The pounding was continuous and terrifying. We had never experienced anything like it during the whole campaign,' wrote a French machine-gunner. '. . . The trench no longer existed, it had been filled with earth. We were crouching in shell-holes, where the mud thrown up by each new explosion covered us more and more. The air was unbreathable. Our own soldiers, the wounded and the blinded, crawling and screaming, kept falling on top of us and died drenching us with their blood . . . Suddenly the enemy artillery lengthened its fire, and almost at once someone shouted: "The Boches are coming!" As if by magic, all of us, still exhausted only a moment ago, faced the enemy immediately, rifle in hand.'

On 10th April, Pétain issued a famous order, acclaiming the French resistance, and ending with the immortal, if unacademic, phrase: *'Courage! On les aura!'* ('We'll get them!') Certainly, it required superhuman courage to keep going. Captain Cochin described the first days of the assault on the Mort Homme in a letter: 'I have returned from the toughest trial I have ever seen — four days and four nights — ninety-six hours — the last two days soaked in icy mud — under terrible bombardment, without any shelter other than the narrowness of the trench, which even then seemed too wide; not a hole, not a dugout, nothing, nothing . . . I arrived there with 175 men, I returned with 34, several half mad.'

It rained solidly for twelve days following the attack of 9th April. The German official history records: 'Water in the trenches came above the knees. The men had not

Left: A French sentry in front of the entrance to Fort Souville

a dry thread on their bodies; there was not a dug-out that could provide dry accommodation. The numbers of sick rose alarmingly.' Despite the mud and misery, persistent French counterattacks had recaptured the whole crest of the Mort Homme by the end of April.

On 3rd May, over 500 German guns opened fire on Côte 304, a front of little over a mile. The bombardment continued for two days and a night. The French, lacking deep shelters after weeks of heavy shelling, suffered appalling casualties. Of one battalion, only three men survived. For over two days no food or supplies could be got through, nor any wounded evacuated. Reinforcements got lost, the units were all jumbled together. After three further days of bitter close combat, Côte 304 finally fell to the Germans. About 10,000 Frenchmen alone had been killed there. By the end of May the Germans had taken the whole of the Mort Homme too. The Bois Bourrus ridge was now overlooked and threatened, and the French artillery positions menacing the right bank neutralized.

This clearing action on the left bank had taken nearly three months and cost the Germans as many lives as all the fighting on the right bank so far; and there were signs that the German casualty rate might now be exceeding that of the French.

The horrors of Verdun

At Verdun, most on either side fell without ever having seen the enemy, under the murderous, unceasing artillery bombardment which came to characterise this battle perhaps more than any other. 'Verdun is terrible,' wrote Sergeant-Major Méléra, 'because man is fighting against material, with the sensation of striking out at empty air'. Fresh troops approaching Verdun heard sounds 'like a gigantic forge that never stopped day or night'. Airmen saw a 'sinister brown belt, a strip of murdered nature. It seems to belong to another world. Every sign of humanity has been swept away.'

All day long the enemy guns worked at levelling the holes the troops had laboriously scraped out the previous night. There was not the chance and no longer the will to bury the dead. The highly-compressed area of the battlefield itself had become a reeking open cemetery. The French writer Duhamel, serving as an army doctor, wrote: 'You eat, you drink beside the dead, you sleep in the midst of the dying, you laugh and sing in the company of corpses.' There were few heroes' deaths; instead, 'these small painful scenes, in obscure corners, of small compass, where you cannot possibly distinguish if the mud is flesh, or the flesh mud.' '. . . to be dismembered, torn to pieces, reduced to pulp, this is a fear that flesh cannot support . . .'

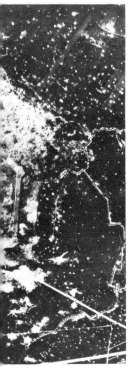

Perhaps the bravest of all were those who were often not fitted for bravery, the runners, the ration-parties, the stretcher-bearers. 'Many would rather endure hunger than make these dangerous expeditions for food,' wrote a German soldier in April. The French *'hommes-soupe'* too, returning at dawn through machine-gun fire, declared they would never do it again; yet the evening saw them 'starting off again on their erratic journey across the fields and gulleys'.

On the right bank, the fighting continued on the south side of Fort Douaumont and round the near-by quarries at Haudromont. The front here never shifted as much as 1,000 yards, and the dense artillery barrage laid down by both sides continued unceasingly. By 1st May the Germans had lost 120,000 at Verdun, the French 133,000. On 21st April the Crown Prince came to the conclusion that 'a decisive success at Verdun could only be assured at the price of heavy sacrifices, out of all proportion to the desired gains'. Knobelsdorf, however, was more resolute than ever and, determined to wrest victory from Verdun, he persuaded Falkenhayn to allow the V Army to undertake a new massive assault on the right bank. Knobelsdorf's iron will had mastered the Crown Prince's change of heart.

There was trouble in the French camp too. Joffre felt that with Pétain's demands for reinforcements – which Pétain saw merely as a necessary rotation of troops – 'the whole French Army would have been absorbed in this battle'; and Pétain was not even planning any offensives. On 19th April, therefore, he decided to promote Pétain to command the Central Group of Armies instead of de Langle de Cary, and to put the confident, eloquent Nivelle, then at the head of the French 3rd Corps at Verdun, in command of the 2nd Army itself. This change was effected on 1st May, Pétain remaining in indirect control of operations from army group HQ at Bar-le-Duc. He was not pleased, fearing increased slaughter which he would be unable to check.

Nivelle was very much under the influence of his 5th Division commander, Mangin – 'the butcher', a tough ex-colonial officer. The idea of recapturing Fort Douaumont obsessed Mangin and he obtained Nivelle's consent to attack it on 22nd May, and obtained a foothold on it; but security had been bad, the Germans had made full preparations, and the French artillery could not touch the inner workings of the thick-hided fort. After two days of slaughter the few remnants of 5th Division crept back to their lines.

Top left: Fort Douaumont before the battle began, showing the extensive fortifications. Bottom left: A reconnaissance photograph of shell-pocked Fort Moulainville at the height of the battle

Mangin was temporarily disgraced; the French line had been badly weakened. French morale at Verdun slumped. As the troops who had fought at Douaumont withdrew to the rear, one of their own officers watched them: 'First came the skeletons of companies occasionally led by a wounded officer, leaning on a stick. All marched, or rather advanced in small steps, zigzagging as if intoxicated . . . They said nothing. They had even lost the strength to complain . . . It seemed as if these mute faces were crying something terrible, the unbelievable horror of their martyrdom.'

On 26th May, Joffre and de Castelnau visited Haig to find out when he would be ready to launch the long-awaited offensive on the Somme, which now, because of the French involvement at Verdun, must be primarily a British responsibility. 'The moment I mentioned August 15th,' wrote Haig in his diary, 'Joffre at once got very excited and shouted that "The French Army would cease to exist if we did nothing till then."' Haig agreed to help the French by making it the 1st July, and 'this calmed the old man . . . They are, indeed, difficult Allies to deal with!'

To France and Germany, Verdun had now become a symbol, an exacting symbol of manhood and honour; and to their soldiers, the battle itself had become the enemy. The original champions, Pétain and the Crown Prince, with their horror of senseless carnage, had lost control of their ruthless subordinates, Nivelle and Knobelsdorf, both determined to fight to the bitterest end. The big German offensive on the right bank in June was fought under these shadows. It seemed there would be no end 'until the last German and the last Frenchman hobbled out of the trenches on crutches to exterminate each other with pocket knives or teeth and finger nails'.

The last German efforts

Knobelsdorf had won round the wavering Falkenhayn to his new offensive, and reinforcements were promised. The Germans now had 2,200 guns at Verdun – though only four worn-out Big Berthas remained to them – to the French 1,777, and everywhere the French margin of withdrawal had become very slender. The Germans were attacking with five divisions on a front of only 3 miles. There would be no surprise: by sheer brute force they intended to gain jumping-off points for the final thrust on Verdun – the Thiaumont stronghold, the Fleury ridge, Fort Souville, and Fort Vaux, in an arc to the south of Douaumont.

Left: A French machine-gun crew advances over a ridge to take up a new position while under heavy German bombardment

The German attack began on 1st June, a glorious summer day, and most of the defences on the approaches to Fort Vaux were quickly overrun. Fort Vaux itself, commanded by the courageous Major Raynal, was attacked first on 2nd June and resisted in an epic defence until the morning of the 7th, when Raynal and his 600 men were forced to surrender through lack of water. For most of this time the Germans had occupied the superstructure of the fort, while the French held out in the heart of it beneath them. A terrible struggle went on day after day in the underground corridors. They fought in pitch darkness, relieved by the flash of exploding grenades, in a shaft 3 feet wide and 5 feet high, with machine-guns and flame-throwers.

Fort Vaux's surrender was offered and accepted with a courtesy which did both sides credit in the surroundings of degradation to which Verdun had reduced the combatants.

Fort Vaux had formed one of the principal buttresses of Pétain's 'line of resistance'. Now even Nivelle began thinking of evacuating the whole right bank. His reserves were down to one brigade. The French artillery was proving less effective: it had lost too many observation posts; and the guns were wearing out. Morale was in a dangerous state; two regiments had broken under the intense German attacks towards Thiaumont. If the Germans had thrust on then, they could almost certainly have broken through to Verdun. Yet on 12th June their offensive unaccountably started to peter out.

It was the Russians, whom the Germans and Austrians had left defeated in the previous autumn, who had now so unexpectedly come to the aid of the French in the hour of crisis. On 4th June, their ablest commander, Brusilov, had launched an attack with his group of armies on the Russian southern wing. The Austrian armies opposing them fell like a pack of cards. But Falkenhayn now realised to his fury—for he and Conrad were by now barely on speaking terms—that it was the Germans again who would have to rush in to the rescue of the Austrians. He therefore sent across three divisions from the West and told the Crown Prince to halt his offensive at Verdun.

The V Army attack, towards Fort Souville and the last heights before Verdun, was eventually resumed on the evening of 22nd June with a heavy barrage of shells containing (for the first time) phosgene gas—the most deadly used in the whole war. The gas was aimed mainly at the French guns in the centre of the line. In the end it did not prove as effective against the French gas-masks as

Right: Verdun: 'A strip of murdered nature. It seems to belong to another world. Every sign of humanity has been swept away'

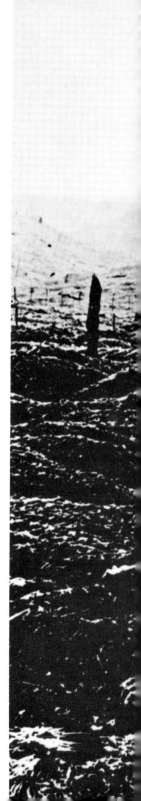

had been expected; and the guns, placed everywhere on high ground, were soon clear of the gas, which sank into the hollows. Knobelsdorf, like other First World War commanders, had not trusted all to this innovation, and he had stopped the gas barrage three hours before his troops attacked, thus giving the French time to recover.

The Germans attacked early on the 23rd on a narrow front with 30,000 men, who included the newly arrived Alpine Corps under von Dellmensingen. They captured Thiaumont and obtained a footing in the village of Fleury, some were even able to fire their machine-guns obliquely into the streets of Verdun itself. But towards the end of that critical day the attack started to ebb: the front was too narrow, the reserves too few, water was desperately scarce, and the French had been given time to regain their balance.

On 24th June, Mangin, returned to favour, started a series of counterattacks on the Bavarians caught in the salient. And on that day, away to the west, the British guns had opened up their barrage north of the Somme. The rumble could be heard at German Supreme Headquarters at Charleville-Mézières: Falkenhayn stopped the flow of ammunition and fresh divisions to Verdun.

The Battle of Verdun was to grind on for another six months; but the crisis was passed.

Knobelsdorf, inflexible, demanded permission for one more attack: they had been so near on 23rd June. Reluctantly Falkenhayn agreed; but it must be out of V Army's own resources. The attack was on 11th July, on an even narrower front, and preceded by a night bombardment of the French artillery with phosgene shells; but this time it was carried on to the moment the German infantry went in. As the gas rolled across the French positions, their guns went silent one by one: the Germans felt wonderfully confident. But when the storm-troops advanced from their shell-holes into the dawn, a barrage of French 75s swept down all along the line. The French gunners, supplied with new and effective gas-masks, had tricked them with their silence.

The battle was nevertheless intense. A group of thirty Germans even managed to gain the outside of Fort Souville, from where they gazed on the twin towers of Verdun Cathedral and the Meuse gleaming through the summer haze between the city streets, like a vision of the Promised Land. But no reinforcements went to their support: the German weapon had been blunted over these five months before Verdun; on this day the last flicker of their hopes dwindled and expired.

Right: In their attempts to consolidate the ground which they had won, German troops move supplies up Mort Homme hill. This was the scene of some of the hardest fighting in the battle

Chapter VII
'A Day of Intense Blue Summer Beauty'

On 1st July 1916, British and French infantry went over the top as the 'Big Push' on the Somme began at last. It was not the best sector to choose for an offensive. The Germans had been entrenched in the chalk downs on the north side of the river since October 1914, everywhere overlooking the Allied positions. Masefield wrote of it: 'Almost in every part of this old front our men had to go up hill to attack . . . The enemy had the look-out posts, with the fine views over France, and the sense of domination. Our men were down below, with no view of anything but of stronghold after stronghold, just up above, being made stronger daily.' Since the British had come into the line here—a much more restless and tiresome opponent than the French had been—the Germans had strengthened their defences to an unprecedented extent. The villages had been fortified, concrete dug-outs and vast dormitories had been sunk 40 feet into the chalk, safe from all but the heaviest British shells, redoubts had been built, and a second, a third, and even in places a fourth line of strong trenches had been dug, to an average depth of four miles. Their line here was, Churchill believed, 'undoubtedly the strongest and most perfectly defended position in the world'.

Joffre, when he had first suggested the Somme, had been influenced far more by the prospects of an integrated Allied attack than by knowledge or consideration of the terrain. The same thing had happened at Loos. Haig evidently agreed without thoroughly examining the lie of the land. But it would, he thought, be good going for cavalry, once the breakthrough was achieved. During the battle, three cavalry divisions, a large slice of the British reserves, were to be kept in constant readiness.

Camouflage behind the British lines was elementary, and all their preparations for the big offensive had been watched in comfort by the enemy. For weeks the Germans had practised rushing their machine-guns up the shafts from the dug-outs. A broad hint dropped in a speech

Left: Men of a British supply party rest in a trench as they move up to the front line during the fighting on the Somme

81

on 2nd June to munition workers by a member of the British government, and reported in the press, added weight to their suspicions. At home on leave, Siegfried Sassoon found that 'even Aunt Evelyn was aware of the impending onslaught'. The Big Push, to come at the end of June, was on everyone's mind. '. . . at Waterloo Station I was visibly reminded that going back for the Push was rather rough on one's relations . . . There were two leave trains and I watched the people coming away after the first one had gone out. Some sauntered away with assumed unconcern; they chatted and smiled. Others hurried past me with a crucified look; I noticed a well-dressed woman biting her gloved fingers; her eyes stared fixedly; she was returning alone to a silent house on a fine Sunday afternoon.'

Starting on 24th June, the preliminary British bombardment lasted a week, two days longer than intended. This great spread, of course, destroyed all hope of surprise, but it succeeded in damaging and unnerving much of the German defence. The number of guns the British had assembled was large, but not nearly large enough. They were spread out evenly, like the infantry, along the whole of the 18-mile British front. At Verdun, the Germans, with far greater numbers of guns, had concentrated their fire on an 8-mile front.

The British attacking force on 1st July totalled fourteen divisions, the French five only. Because of Verdun, for the first time the British were making the main effort on the Western Front. The two British divisions on the northern flank, belonging to 7th Corps, in Allenby's 3rd Army, were only engaged on a diversionary attack against the village of Gommécourt, and had purposely disclosed their preparations; but the Germans were ready all down the front of attack.

The main force of twelve British divisions, attacking from the village of Hébuterne southward to Maricourt, some 2,000 yards short of the Somme, made up Rawlinson's 4th Army, which had been formed here when 3rd Army was slipped northwards to relieve the French 10th Army in March.

The French, in the south, were placed astride the Somme. On their left, adjoining the British, Balfourier's 20th Corps, which had tipped the scales at Verdun at the end of February, was attacking along the north bank of the Somme. All five of the French divisions, and their reserves, came under Fayolle's 6th Army.

Facing the British and French were five divisions of von Stein's XIV Reserve Corps north of the Somme, and one division of von Pannwitz's XVII Corps south of the river. They all came under General Fritz von Below's II Army, which had its HQ at St Quentin. Not being able to extort

reserves from Falkenhayn, despite the evidence accumulating that an offensive against his front was being prepared, Below had urged on the further strengthening of the defence lines along the chalk downs north of the river. He had also noted the French reinforcement south of the Somme, but Falkenhayn estimated that the French would not have the strength to attack on both sides of the river: he had misinterpreted Pétain's rotation of units through Verdun, and believed that their divisions there were only withdrawn, like his own, after complete exhaustion.

Of the fourteen British divisions, eleven were either Territorials who had agreed to serve in France, or were made up from Kitchener's New Armies – the volunteers of 1915. Of these, George V declared proudly: 'Isn't it *perfectly* wonderful? No man could have done it but Lord K. People kept saying he was going to work in the wrong way, but *he* knew better. *He* was right after all.'

'Unvarying parade-ground formations'

Because, however, of the poor organisation at home and the need for men to man the trenches in France (in which the British were still very prodigal), the New Army troops were barely trained. They had been taught little more than to advance in unvarying parade-ground formations – straight lines with two to three paces between each man and a hundred yards between each rank of the assault waves: the infantry, they were led to believe, 'would only have to walk over No Man's Land and take possession'. It might have been Dettingen, and the machine-gun a dream of fiction. The paradox was that these men, with their fresh enthusiasm, their wide range of non-military experience, and their high average intelligence, were just those who would well have learnt the more complex tactics of infiltration which the Germans and French were evolving at Verdun. But the generals would not trust them. Haig, it is true, had at one point suggested that the infantry should advance in detachments, not waves – after the manner of the Germans at Verdun – but his army commanders had opposed him.

Haig (as usual) was aiming at a breakthrough after a short bombardment, with his cavalry in attendance, despite his weakness in heavy guns for such a purpose. Rawlinson, who would carry out the attack, thought this could not be done. He wanted a long bombardment to

Left: The men of the New Armies who were massacred on the Somme. Their commanders failed to take advantage of their enthusiasm and intelligence to evolve new tactics, and sent them forward in parade-ground formation to be slaughtered

smash the first-line defences and a slow advance in stages. The result was a compromise—a long bombardment, destroying any last element of surprise, followed by an infantry attack too evenly spread to break through this heavily fortified line, yet with ambitious objectives.

French initial successes

It was the French south of the Somme who achieved surprise by going in to the attack two hours later than the British and their own comrades on the north bank. This delay reinforced the German belief that the French were not in a position to attack south of the river. So they were able to push on beyond their first day's objectives in several places. The French junior officers and NCOs had learnt their lessons from Vimy Ridge, Champagne, and Verdun, and crossed No Man's Land in groups, loosely spaced, dashing forward between the craters their own artillery had made, and giving each other cover as they advanced. Their artillery had been most destructive: here it was flat land, and the German front trenches had been totally obliterated, the entrances to their forward dug-outs closed, and their artillery silenced. The French had their eyes on Péronne, 4 miles on.

The French 20th Corps, north of the river, had also had their way through the first German lines eased for them by their artillery, including the 240-mm mortars and the new 400-mm 'super-heavies' with which Foch, still commanding the Northern Group of Armies, had equipped Fayolle's army: '. . . nearly all the deep dug-outs in the first position were blown in, only a few specially deep ones were still partly serviceable. The garrison lay mainly in shell and mine craters.'

Where the French were able to dash forward, take cover, split into groups, and make another dash, the British soldiers, these brave but mistrusted soldiers of the New Armies, advancing as ordered in straight, vulnerable lines, and keeping above ground—that is, never doing anything so ungentlemanly as to crawl or take cover—would not even be able to run. Each man was weighed down by a minimum load of 66 lbs. They carried into battle their personal kit—including a spare pair of socks—water bottles, a day's rations, two gas masks, mess tins and field dressings, as well as rifle, bayonet, 220 rounds of ammunition, and an entrenching tool. Half of them carried a shovel or pick as well. Some also carried hand grenades or trench mortar bombs, increasing their load to 85 or 90 lbs. The British Official

Far right: The battlefield of the Somme showing the stages of the advance. The initial attack was launched by the British 4th and French 6th Armies astride the Somme. Right from top: The Allied commanders: Haig, Rawlinson, Gough, and Fayolle

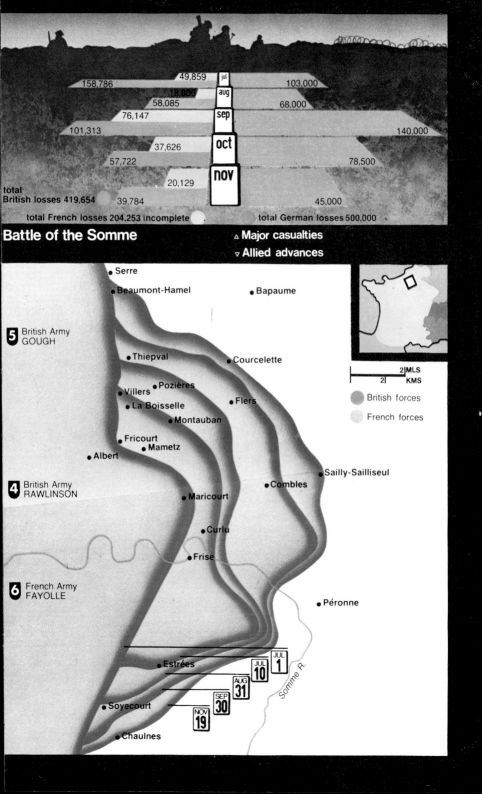

Battle of the Somme

History says: 'The total weight . . . made it difficult to
get out of a trench, impossible to move much quicker
than a slow walk, or to rise and lie down quickly. This
overloading of the men is by many infantry officers regarded as one of the principal reasons for the heavy losses
and failure of their battalions; for their men could not
get through the machine-gun zone with sufficient speed.'
But they were at last wearing steel helmets, belatedly
— and reluctantly — following the example of the French:
'We have all been served out with the new shrapnel
helmet, and now we look like so many Tweedledees,'
said one British officer, '. . . the tin hats . . . are jolly good
things, nevertheless, and if they had been started earlier
would have saved thousands of lives.' The Germans, too,
at this time were changing over to their plain, 'coal-
scuttle' steel helmets, in place of the ornamental spiked
helmet of the first years of the war.

Where the French had at their backs a concentration
of artillery that could be relied on to erase the enemy's
trenches, explode his wire into shreds, block his dug-outs,
and destroy the positions from which the surviving
machine-gunners could fire with any advantage, the
British, despite the duration of their barrage, found
themselves on the eve of the attack still faced by long
stretches of uncut wire. A sergeant on the 8th Corps
front even reported: 'I don't think they've been trying
to cut the wire in this area.' On the 10th Corps front,
beneath the village of Thiepval, they could see that many
of the original belts of wire — often 40 yards deep — were
untouched. Even divisional commanders knew this, but
somehow the news was not allowed to filter higher.
Horne, 15th Corps commander, told Haig: 'Wire very
well cut.' Pulteney, 3rd Corps commander, was 'quite
satisfied' with the wire cutting. Rawlinson did not know
the true position, nor did Haig. Haig, with his implicit
belief that heavy artillery must destroy wire and trenches,
evidently did not think of asking further. He merely
states in his diary on 30th June: 'The wire has never
been so well cut, nor the artillery preparation so thorough.'

Here was one of those gaps in the chain of communication which could occur in the BEF. Too much assurance
at the top, for one thing, tempted those who were able
to see to turn a blind eye, to note the favourable reports
rather than the warnings. There was the separation between GHQ staff and the front line: Haig and his staff
seemed to have difficulty in finding time to visit further
forward than corps HQs. And at the time of the Somme,
the mistrust between the regulars and the New Army
volunteers was considerable. The impact of the prolonged
and costly war had still not broken down the barriers in
which the Regular Army enclosed itself.

The British attack

So at 7.30 on the morning of 1st July, which was to be a broiling hot day after the recent wet and cloudy weather, nearly 100,000 British soldiers left their trenches and moved forward towards the German wire at a steady walk. 'They got going without delay; no fuss, no shouting, no running, everything solid and thorough—just like the men themselves. Here and there a boy would wave his hand to me as I shouted good luck to them through my megaphone. And all had a cheery face. Most were carrying loads. Fancy advancing against heavy fire with a big roll of barbed wire on your shoulders!'

The moment the bombardment lifted, the German troops 'clambered up the steep shafts leading from the dug-outs to daylight and ran for the nearest shell craters. The machine-guns were pulled out of the dug-outs and hurriedly placed in position, their crews dragging the heavy ammunition boxes up the steps and out to the guns. A rough firing line was thus rapidly established. As soon as they were in position, a series of extended lines of British infantry were seen moving forward from the British trenches. The first line appeared to continue without end to right and left. It was quickly followed by a second line, then a third and fourth. They came on at a steady, easy pace as if expecting to find nothing alive in our front trenches.'

The northernmost corps of 4th Army's attack, Hunter-Weston's 8th Corps, was faced with the most difficult terrain, in particular opposite the fortified village of Beaumont-Hamel. It was about this corps that Haig had the most doubts.

On 8th Corps's left, 31st Division was meant to capture the hamlet of Serre. Some who found gaps in the wire were caught by enfilading machine-gun fire; others were scythed down before they reached the wire. 'The extended lines started in excellent order,' says the British Official History, 'but gradually melted away. There was no wavering or attempting to come back, the men fell in their ranks, mostly before the first hundred yards of No Man's Land had been crossed.' Some small detachments did penetrate the German lines here, but were then lost to view: their graves were found months later. By the early afternoon, 31st Division had lost 3,600 officers and men, of whom only eight were prisoners.

In the centre of 8th Corps, 4th Division attacked up the Redan Ridge and its redoubt, on the north side of Beaumont-Hamel. They met unexpectedly strong fire from undestroyed trenches and fortified positions. Some reached the support trench behind, but were then over-

Left: One of the villages shattered by British bombardment

come by Germans swarming out of their dug-outs. The second British wave ran into intense artillery fire crossing No Man's Land, and the German guns had started to bombard the British trenches too. A small force was able to take advantage of a premature explosion in the Heiden-kopf strongpoint, and penetrated to the support area and beyond, but was taken in the rear.

To ease the southern approach to Beaumont-Hamel, a mine had been set under the Germans' Hawthorn Re-doubt; but the strange decision had been made to blow it at ten minutes before zero hour, and lift the artillery barrage in this sector at the same moment, which gave the German machine-gunners time to reoccupy the crater before the British could get there. The blowing of the mine had set the alarm, and the Germans were ready to receive the first wave of the British 29th Division; the second wave, crossing No Man's Land half an hour later, could see the uncut wire ahead of them festooned by the bodies of their fellows. Of the Newfoundland Regi-ment, 710 fell in a few minutes.

During the afternoon, local efforts were made to reach the men still fighting in the German trenches along the 8th Corps front, but to no avail. The corps had lost 14,000 officers and men, without even broaching their main objective, Beaumont-Hamel.

Morland's 10th Corps, attacking south of the river Ancre, was aiming, like 3rd Corps on its right, to reach the high ground beyond Pozières, the northern part of the ridge which was Haig's first objective. On 10th Corps's left, the right-hand brigade of the 36th (Ulster) Division, led by the Inniskillings, achieved a remarkable success. They advanced at a good pace through the tumbled Ger-man wire and across the fire trench between the Ancre and Thiepval, keeping well up behind their own barrage. Within an hour they had advanced a mile up to the crest of the ridge and captured the complex of German trenches there called the Schwaben Redoubt. But since, by Haig's orders following the heavy losses of field officers in 1915, battalion commanders and their seconds-in-command were not allowed to go in with the first wave, and com-munications with the rear had broken down, the Ulster-men, lacking leadership, failed to consolidate their success before the Germans recovered their balance — though they too were slow and bungled the bringing up of reinforcements. Before withdrawing under cover of dark-ness, their ammunition exhausted, the Ulsters' reserve

Top right: Artillery in action during the preliminary bombard-ment. The British had assembled more guns than ever before.
Bottom left: The troops go over the top. 'They got going without delay', advancing steadily into the machine-gun fire hampered by cumbersome packs which often weighed more than 80 lbs

brigade had even gone on to capture a part of the German second line and to hold it for a time, although, advancing too fast, they had first run into their own barrage. The 36th Division clung to the German front line, but their initial success had turned out disastrously through inadequate support.

The 32nd Division, on the right, was attacking Thiepval village. '. . . my eyes are riveted on a sight I shall never see again. It is the 32nd Division at its best,' wrote a British eye-witness. 'I see rows upon rows of British soldiers lying dead, dying or wounded, in No Man's Land. Here and there I see an officer urging on his followers . . . Again I look southward . . . and perceive heaped up masses of British corpses suspended on the German wire in front of the Thiepval stronghold, while live men rush forward in orderly procession to swell the weight of numbers in the spider's web.' A small body of Lancashire Fusiliers got through to the village, but were then cut off by defenders emerging from their dug-outs behind them. The knowledge that these men might still be in Thiepval prevented Morland, 10th Corps commander, from shelling the village in the afternoon, despite the trouble its defences were giving.

The Highland Light Infantry were attacking the Leipzig Redoubt, a chalk quarry on the south side of Thiepval. They crossed No Man's Land behind their pipers. One battalion entered the German trenches through extensive gaps in the wire, but concealed machine-guns then pinned them down. The other battalion had found no gaps in the wire and large numbers were caught on it by enemy fire. The 10th Corps's losses were 9,000.

In Pulteney's 3rd Corps sector south of Thiepval, 8th Division attacked opposite Ovillers, which was held by Swabians of the 180th Regiment: '. . . when the leading British line was within a hundred yards, the rattle of [German] machine-gun and rifle fire broke out along the whole line of shell-holes. Some fired kneeling so as to get a better target over the broken ground, whilst others, in the excitement of the moment, stood up regardless of their own safety, to fire into the crowd of men in front of them . . . a mass of shells from the German batteries in the rear tore through the air and burst among the advancing lines. Whole sections seemed to fall, and the rear formations, moving in close order, quickly scattered. The advance rapidly crumpled under this hail of shells and bullets. All along the line men could be seen throwing up their arms and collapsing, never to move again . . . The British soldier, however, has no lack of courage . . . The extended lines, though badly shaken and with many gaps, now came on all the faster. Instead of a leisurely walk they covered the ground in short

rushes at the double . . . the infantry rushed forward with fixed bayonets . . . Again and again the extended lines of British infantry broke against the German defence like waves against a cliff, only to be beaten back.' The 8th Division casualties were 218 officers out of 300 and 5,274 men out of 8,500; of these, 1,927 were killed outright. The German 180th Regiment had opposed them with about 1,800 men, and had lost 8 officers and 273 soldiers.

British successes of the day
Horne's 15th Corps sector, opposite Fricourt and Mametz, was the watershed between the successes of the French on the right flank and the terrible British defeat unfolding on their left. The 7th Division attack on the village of Mametz suffered initially from machine-gun fire as the British troops sought ways through the wire, which had not all been cut. They entered Mametz and were driven out again; but in the afternoon they broke in once more after bombardment. By evening the Mametz defences had been broken. To the left, although as the Germans admitted, 'the trenches and obstacles, the weaker dug-outs and also the best observation posts were nearly completely destroyed' by the long British bombardment, the men of 21st Division were badly held up by a few machine-guns as they tried to move round to the north of the strongly held village of Fricourt; and in the afternoon, when ordered to 'press home the attack as planned', most of them never got across No Man's Land.

For Congreve's 13th Corps, the French advance on the south flank, and above all their generous artillery support, had been a considerable help. They were through the village of Montauban before mid-day. It had been pounded by the French 240s for a week, and its cellars were full of German dead. Congreve was however unwilling to push on further, though the way seemed clear and Balfourier on his right urged it. He was sticking instead to the letter of Rawlinson's orders, which underlined the consolidation of objectives gained; and 15th Corps on his left was lagging behind. So Balfourier's 20th Corps could not advance either.

In the extreme north, the 7th Corps diversion against Gommécourt fared no better than the main attack. The German II Guards Reserve Division opposite the British 46th Division was well prepared. Bunching to pass through the few gaps in the wire, the British were terribly exposed to the German machine-gun and rifle fire. On their right, the 56th (London) Division had more

Left: In a few places in the south the British did make a small amount of progress and captured about 2,500 German prisoners

success and gained its first objectives, but lack of reinforcements and ammunition prevented them from holding out against strong German counterattacks. The 7th Corps, at immense cost, had fulfilled its task to the letter: to divert onto themselves 'the fire of artillery and infantry which might otherwise be directed against the left flank of the main attack near Serre'. To this end, 7,000 men had fallen opposite Gommécourt.

The number of German prisoners taken reads, from south to north, like a falling barometer of success. The two and a half French corps took 6,000 prisoners, as well as destroying the whole of the German 121st Division's artillery. The British 13th Corps, which shared in the French success, took 934 prisoners; 15th Corps, the watershed, 517; 3rd Corps, 32; 10th Corps, including the Ulstermen's lunge forward, 478; 8th Corps, 22.

Total British casualties on that 'blackest' day were 57,470 – nearly half the infantry engaged – including almost 20,000 men killed. They were the heaviest losses in British history. At Verdun, by comparison, the French, in the whole of their worst month (June) barely exceeded these figures.

Kitchener's men, these one-time civilians, had borne this day with incredible fortitude, suffering losses which might have broken a professional army. Spears, then British Liaison Officer with the French 6th Army, was in a position to see how needless much of this sacrifice had been: '. . . my memory was seared with the picture of the French and British attacking together on the Somme . . . the British rigid and slow, advancing as at an Aldershot parade in lines that were torn and ripped by the German guns, while the French tactical formations, quick and elastic, secured their objectives with trifling loss. It had been a terrible spectacle. The German artillery, with targets no gunner could resist, neglected the more dangerous but invisible French groups and concentrated on the British. For long minutes this line or that of the many waves succeeding each other was completely invisible in the smoke of explosions a mile long, and when seen again, though showing gaps of hundreds of yards where there had been men before, was perceived to be slowly advancing at the same even pace. As a display of bravery it was magnificent, as an example of tactics its very memory made one shudder.'

This day – 'a day of an intense blue summer beauty' – was but the first of a battle which was to drag on into November.

Left: 'Gassed and Wounded', a painting by Eric Kennington

The new birds of prey

It was in the skies over Verdun and the Somme that one of the most important weapons to be developed during the First World War came into its own. The aeroplane had been used for reconnaissance and skirmishing in 1914-15, but during their preparations for the Verdun offensive the Germans first used massed aircraft to sweep French reconnaissance flights out of the sky. The French broke this strangle-hold by concentrating their aircraft and throwing them into battle as the famous *Groupe de Cigognes* (the Storks) led by aces such as Guynemer (**below**). The German answer, the 'Flying Circus' developed by Boelcke and Immelmann, was ineffective over Verdun, but over the Somme their co-ordinated fighter tactics enabled Boelcke's squadrons to shoot down more than 123 Allied aircraft in one month for the loss of only 27. Nevertheless the powerful Royal Flying Corps (**left**) kept supremacy for the British

Chapter VIII
The Somme and Verdun Grind On

Haig did not at first realise the extent of the Somme losses on 1st July, nor the great quantity of ammunition expended; so that the attacks were continued on the 2nd and 3rd, though with less conviction. He saw, however, that the path was blocked in the north, and urged a reluctant Rawlinson to follow up on his right flank rather than try to increase the small footholds round Thiepval in the centre.

On the afternoon of 3rd July, Joffre and Foch — the latter directing the French effort on the Somme — came over to see Haig. There was strong disagreement over the immediate British objective, and Joffre excitedly *ordered* Haig to attack Thiepval and Pozières, instead of concentrating on the Longueval sector behind Montauban in the south. This lapse from good form on Joffre's part gave Haig an opportunity for providing a satisfactory display of 'keeping calm', and seems to have hardened his resolve to push forward his attack towards Longueval.

Both 15th Corps and 13th Corps in the south, however, were showing lamentable caution in the face of a German defence which was seriously shaken, and this meant that the French 20th Corps dare not pursue its advantage either. But south of the Somme the French captured the second line and the high ground overlooking Péronne.

Haig had found that the initial (rather low) estimate of casualties suffered on 1st July — 40,000 — 'cannot be considered severe in view of the numbers engaged, and the length of front attacked'. Rawlinson, on the other hand, seems to have been considerably affected by the losses, and therefore decided to launch his major attack on the Longueval Ridge at the first light of dawn, his men having crossed the dangerous spaces of No Man's Land during the night, guided by marker tapes. The French considered it all far too risky — 'an attack organised for amateurs by amateurs' — and refused to take part, though Fayolle offered to supply an artillery barrage to protect the British right flank. But Rawlinson felt that a bold step was necessary in order to gain the German second

Left: A British guide waits in the ruins to take out a patrol

97

line, before they had time to make it as strong as the first line had been. He had his way, and the attack was made at dawn on 14th July.

The troops – under 13th and 15th Corps for the main attack – many of them replacements from other army sectors, were keyed up to the adventure as they waited on their markers in the dark of night. 'All the time I was saying to myself "You're there. You're there, boy. Right in the middle of No Man's Land and no one can see you, no one's firing. You're going to get away with it – right up under the barrage into Jerry's trenches before he knows it."' Now they moved on in silence towards the enemy line. Before they attacked, their own artillery let loose a hurricane bombardment of five minutes only, and the troops swept into the dazed German trenches.

The operation was brilliantly carried out, and the German second-line trenches were breached for $3\frac{1}{2}$ miles, from Bazentin-le-Petit Wood to the edge of Longueval. 'Ils ont osé,' telephoned the French Liaison Officer excitedly. 'Ils ont réussi.'

On the right flank, further advance into Delville Wood was bitterly contested. This was the South African Brigade's moment of immortality, in the holocaust of the blazing wood, before the Germans recaptured it. On the left flank the opportunity was lost of walking on into High Wood (Bois des Foureaux), on its commanding rise, which reconnaissance showed was empty: it was to be left for the cavalry to exploit. The cavalry was slow in coming up over the cratered ground; and even then the two corps commanders, Horne and Congreve, procrastinated. When at last the cavalry were sent in, pennants fluttering across the ripening corn, to take the wood with the battle-weary 7th Division, nine hours had been lost. German reinforcements were coming up, the British occupied the wood only precariously and were driven out next day.

Sassoon watched the men of 7th Division coming out of the line after fighting for a week in High Wood. 'The field guns came first, with nodding men sitting stiffly on weary horses, followed by wagons and limbers and field-kitchens. After this rumble of wheels came the infantry, shambling, limping, straggling and out of step . . . with an almost spectral appearance, the lurching brown figures flitted past with slung rifles and heads bent forward under basin-helmets. . . . It was all in the day's work – an exhausted Division returning from the Somme Offensive – but for me it was as though I had watched an army of ghosts.' It was to be two months before the British cleared High Wood.

Right: British troops set out for the deadly march to the enemy trenches. Only once, at Longueval, did they try different tactics

Attrition on the Somme

The turn of the tide at High Wood on the evening of 14th July marked the general decline of the British impetus and the strengthening of the German resistance, in numbers and organisation. Haig himself was affected by the disappointment of it. Artillery ammunition was causing him concern; without massive artillery support no offensive seemed possible; all that was left to him was to grind on, to push relentlessly forward in a drawn-out battle of attrition, the kind of fighting he understood best. The arrival on the Somme of the 1st Australian Division gave the opportunity to increase the British pressure. While the Australians, brought in under Gough's Reserve Army in the northern sector, attacked Pozières on 23rd July, Rawlinson's 4th Army renewed their attempt to reach High Wood – utterly in vain, though they at last secured Delville Wood and the adjacent village of Longueval. The Australians captured Pozières, but strong German counterattacks contained them. As further Australian divisions from Birdwood's Anzac Corps arrived from Flanders, they were thrown into the bitter fighting on the high ridge round Pozières, which swayed backwards and forwards indecisively for six weeks, until the Australians were relieved on 4th September, having lost 23,000 men. One of their steadiest officers wrote: 'We have just come out of a place so terrible that . . . a raving lunatic could never imagine the horror of the last thirteen days.' The Australian Official History remarks: 'To throw the several parts of an army corps, brigade after brigade . . . twenty times in succession against one of the strongest points in the enemy's defence, may certainly be described as "methodical", but the claim that it was economic is entirely unjustified.'

On the 4th Army front there were similar slogging attacks towards the village of Guillemont throughout the latter part of July and the whole of August – the 'terrible road into Guillemont, straight, desolate, swept by fire', measured now in weeks of suffering and death. A young German officer describes the position his platoon held there as 'nothing but a series of enormous shell-holes filled with pieces of uniform, weapons, and dead bodies'.

And with Guillemont taken on 3rd September came the same effort against Ginchy.

The French south of the Somme had slowed down as the German resistance increased and they had come to a halt on the river bank opposite Péronne.

Left: French assault troops reach the German line at Verdun. While the British persisted in sending their men forward in successive lines and in making no attempt to take cover, the French and Germans at Verdun were evolving new offensive tactics using small groups moving independently under cover

The fall of Falkenhayn

The Germans, on their side, had maintained their bitter defence and their incessant and costly counterattacks only with the help of hurried compromises in reinforcement and some shuffling of the command structure. Falkenhayn, taken in by Haig's simple preliminary feints, had thought the Somme preparations a diversion for a bigger offensive opposite Arras. The reinforcement which Below and his II Army therefore needed came with grudging reluctance, and the first few days of July shook the Germans considerably. Von Gallwitz was now brought in as II Army commander south of the Somme, while Below commanded a new I Army north of the river. New groups were formed under corps commanders – von Armin and von Gossler north of the river, von Quast to the south. On 28th August, Crown Prince Rupprecht, a very able soldier, was given command of a new Army Group embracing his own VI Army opposite Arras and these two armies, I and II, on the Somme.

The Germans had opposed the onslaught of 1st July with thirty-three battalions, of which twelve had been effectively destroyed. The inaction of Horne and Congreve on the following days allowed Below to bring his front-line strength up to forty battalions by the time of the attack of 14th July on his second line. Throughout July, German artillery replacements and reinforcements were brought in, from the rear, from Crown Prince Rupprecht's army, and from V Army at Verdun: on 11th July Falkenhayn had ordered V Army to remain purely on the defensive. In the air, three flights were transferred from Verdun in the hope of curtailing the Royal Flying Corps's supremacy, which was so vital for artillery observation. These German aircraft were Captain Boelcke's new 'Flying Circus' (or, more correctly, 'Pursuit Squadron'), an early attempt at evolving co-ordinated fighter tactics.

The Somme battle, however bitter its failures and its losses, had most certainly contributed to the relief of Verdun, nipping off Knobelsdorf's intensive assault early in July on the last ring of forts guarding the city. The Germans' inability to withstand the Allies' slowly grinding pressure of the Somme and their need to call off the decisive attack at Verdun had impressed Roumania to the extent that on 27th August she entered the war on the Allies' side. This action in fact did neither her nor the Allies any good, as her army was quickly crushed by the Germans and Austrians, but it was the event which finally brought about the fall of Falkenhayn. On 29th August, the Kaiser, hitherto his loyal supporter, re-

Right: The aftermath of the battle. French troops examine some of the German artillery which was captured during their attacks

102

placed him by the joint team of Hindenburg and Ludendorff. Falkenhayn at least had his revenge on Roumania, by being the instrument of her defeat in the autumn as commander of the German IX Army.

When Falkenhayn had visited the Somme front on 3rd July, after the first onslaught, he had angrily reaffirmed that 'the first principle of position warfare must be to yield not one foot of ground; and if it be lost to retake it immediately by counterattack, even to the use of the last man'. This led the Germans, even though it was no Verdun they were defending, into an inflexibility of tactics and a crescendo of casualties which almost matched those of the British. It was this aspect which now struck Hindenburg and Ludendorff on their first acquaintance, early in September, with the unique problems of the Western Front. Ludendorff wrote of this visit: '. . . The loss of ground up to date appeared to me of little importance in itself. We could stand that; but the question how this, and the progressive falling-off of our fighting power of which it was symptomatic, was to be prevented, was of immense importance . . . The Field-Marshal and I could for the moment only ask that the front line should be held more lightly, the deep underground works be destroyed, and all trenches and posts be given up if the retention of them were unnecessary to the maintenance of the position as a whole, and likely to be the cause of heavy losses.' This was indeed a reversal of Falkenhayn's principles.

Haig's 'Secret Weapon'

On the British side, too, an uncomfortably critical spirit was being generated. In June, Kitchener had been drowned when his ship was torpedoed, and Lloyd George, ever suspicious of the generals, had succeeded him at the War Office. Now he was plaguing Robertson with searching questions on the Somme losses, which Robertson was passing on to Haig, who hid his head in the Somme chalk: 'I have no intention of going before the War Committee while this battle is going on.'

Haig still hoped to break out on the Somme. He was planning an offensive to do this for mid-September, and the slow, relentless clearing of the Pozières and Longueval ridges was preparatory to this. Fayolle helped loyally by capturing a substantial part of the German line south-east of le Forest and cutting the main road from Bapaume to Péronne at Bouchavesnes.

For this coming offensive, for this final attempt to break out through the German third line of defences into

Right: The second line of British troops advances during the battle of Morval *(top)*. A machine-gun fires in support *(bottom)*

open country and reach Bapaume, Haig decided to throw in a bizarre new invention called the 'tank', the first fifty-nine of which had just arrived in France. All warnings and entreaties from inventors, sponsors, and Cabinet ministers not to use the first few untried vehicles prematurely, not to throw away their secret before there were enough to be launched into a mass assault on the German trenches, were ruthlessly disregarded.

Tanks—that was just a cover name in those days—had been evolved since the beginning of 1915 as Britain's answer to the stalemate of the trench barrier on the Western Front: a mobile fortress to outwit the machine-gun, heavy enough to crush the barbed wire, with caterpillar traction to overcome the trenches themselves and the shell-torn ground. From the start it was Churchill who saw the need and the possibilities and kept the idea alive. The design of Major Swinton, a staff officer in France, was the one developed in the end, and the first machine made satisfactory tests in February 1916. Kitchener regarded it as 'a pretty mechanical toy but of very limited military value'; but his judgement was disregarded and production of 150 'caterpillars' went ahead, Haig having pressed for a supply for France. There were two models: 'males' carrying two 6-pounder guns and four Hotchkiss machine-guns; and 'females' carrying one Hotchkiss and four Vickers machine-guns. The French too were working on these lines, but were less far advanced.

Haig, with his attack of 15th September pending and nearly sixty tanks in France, wrote to Robertson: 'Even if I do not get so many as I hope, I shall use what I have got, as I cannot wait any longer for them, and it would be folly not to use any means at my disposal in what is likely to be our crowning effort for this year.' He was, in effect, going to use up the tanks as he had used up the New Armies—for valid reasons, but prematurely, untried, without thought, preparation, or training. Churchill was 'shocked at the proposal to expose this tremendous secret to the enemy upon such a petty scale and as a mere make-weight to what I was sure could only be an indecisive operation'.

On 15th September, only thirty-two tanks reached the assembly area in working order; twenty-four went into battle, and most of these broke down, became bogged, or were knocked out. They were, in any case, put in piecemeal, contrary to all the principles laid down by Swinton and his tank men.

On the extreme left of the main attack, the Canadian 2nd Division from Gough's Reserve Army successfully advanced up the Bapaume road and captured Courcelette.

Right: Used before they were ready, British tanks moving up

106

Their allocation of tanks moved forward bravely, but always in the rear of the infantry.

The 15th (Scottish) Division went forward with great boldness and took Martinpuich. There one surviving tank did useful work clearing trenches, but was hardly a spearhead. The 50th (Northumbrian) Division were held up on their right by machine-gun fire from the ever menacing High Wood, which 47th (London) Division took several hours to clear at last, its three tanks proving more a hindrance among the tree stumps than a help. This delay limited much of 3rd Corps's advance, and they nowhere approached the German third line.

It was 15th Corps that had the success this day, and the capture and holding of the fortress village of Flers, on the German third line, by 41st Division in the centre of the corps's attack, marked the first triumph of the tank. It was, in fact, four tanks which shared this success; and Lieutenant Hastie's in particular, advancing up the main street of Flers at a critical moment, 'fire spitting from its guns', its crew secure against shrapnel and machine-guns, drew spontaneous cheers from the infantry as it led them on to the last German defences.

The 14th Corps were seriously obstructed by a German defence position, the 'Quadrilateral'. The corps's sixteen tanks were just the job for tackling it; but of those which actually started, several found that the unaccustomed shell-torn terrain confused their already restricted field of vision, so that they quickly lost their sense of direction and one at least advanced on the British lines, firing on its own troops. There were similar occurrences in other corps's sectors. German resistance had again proved just too strong for a breakthrough; but only just—even those stuttering, inexperienced tanks, if they had been massed in one sector only, instead of spread about in diminished threes, would have led the infantry, and the waiting cavalry too, right through to Bapaume.

The Somme peters out

That evening the rain started, and continued. The British held most of the crest of the ridge now, looking down on the Germans. On 26th September, Thiepval, a thorn in the flesh ever since 1st July, fell at last.

The autumn rains combined with the shelling to make the roads and the battlefield a sea of deep mud; but still Haig soldiered on, persuading himself that the exhausted Germans might yet break. In November, a soldier wrote: 'Whoever it is we are relieving, they have already gone. The trench is empty . . . Corpses lie along the parados,

Right: German prisoners captured during the battle of Morval

rotting in the wet; every now and then a booted foot appears jutting out of the trench. The mud makes it all but impassable, and now, sunk in it up to the knees, I have the momentary terror of never being able to pull myself out . . . This is the very limit of endurance.' Finally, in a massive attack between 13th and 19th November, Gough, whose Reserve Army was now up-graded to become the 5th, captured Beaumont-Hamel, another bitter pill left over from the initial assault. The last attack had been made.

The advantage the British had won in September, by gaining the crest of the ridge, had been steadily thrown away in October and November by pushing on downhill into the further plain. Now they no longer overlooked the Germans, and faced the winter in a new set of flooded trenches.

The French counter-offensive at Verdun

Disturbed enough by what they saw of the Somme battlefield, at Verdun Hindenburg and Ludendorff were horrified: 'Battles there,' wrote Hindenburg, 'exhausted our forces like an open wound. Moreover, it was obvious that in any case the enterprise had become hopeless . . . The battlefield was a regular hell and regarded as such by the troops.' And Ludendorff added: 'Our losses were too heavy for us.' The German losses at Verdun now totalled 281,333; the French, 315,000.

Rebelling over the continued heavy, nervous fighting at Verdun in July and August, though it was defensive on both sides, the Crown Prince had at last persuaded the Kaiser to remove Knobelsdorf to a distant command on 23rd August. Now Hindenburg and Ludendorff ordered that all attacks at Verdun should be stopped. Pétain too, on his side, angered by another fiasco of Mangin's and wishing to gather forces together for a powerful counter-offensive at Verdun in the autumn, stopped the French attacks. An uneasy calm fell over the battlefield.

Pétain, Nivelle, and Mangin now worked smoothly together preparing the autumn offensive. The objective was Fort Douaumont itself, one of the most powerful symbols of the Verdun battle. The French would attack on a narrow front with three divisions in front, followed by another three, with two more in reserve. Pétain assembled 650 guns in this sector, half of which were heavies, against 450-500 German guns. Most dramatic of all, the French had brought up two of their new 400-mm railway guns into position behind the Verdun front.

Nivelle was a gunner, and he organised a creeping barrage for the attack — an elaboration of a technique

Left: French troops shelter during a counterattack at Verdun

111

tried out by the British 15th Corps on the Somme on 1st July. To ensure liaison, special deep telephone lines were laid. The infantry were trained for this task to the highest pitch of perfection on a simulated battlefield, till they could have walked up to Fort Douaumont blindfold.

Everywhere in the French camp there was a new confidence. The spirit in the Crown Prince's army was very different. The Germans had lost the initiative and knew they were about to be attacked. Senior officers no longer had a sense of purpose, the troops were exhausted: many had spent the hot summer on the Somme, others had been too long at Verdun. They were being bombarded steadily by the French, and the continuous autumn rain, with frosts at night, demoralised them further. There had never been so many desertions.

The French preliminary bombardment began on 19th October. It lifted on the 22nd, long enough for the German field guns, thinking the attack imminent, to reveal their positions; then it descended again as savagely as ever, with the German batteries a special target. On the 23rd, the new French 400-mm guns started to bombard Fort Douaumont, destroying its reinforced crust and starting dangerous fires within.

The French attacked on the morning of 24th October in a thick mist, which added to the German surprise and discomfort. Fort Douaumont was only thinly held and fell with little resistance. Success accompanied the French everywhere, and on this one day they reconquered ground which the Germans had taken four and a half months to gain.

On 2nd November the French re-took Fort Vaux. On 15th December, in the bitterest winter weather, they pushed the Germans back a good 2 miles beyond Douaumont. The French losses in these counteroffensives had been severe, but the German losses had been heavier; and in December alone 11,000 German prisoners, from all five divisions engaged, and 115 guns were taken at Verdun. So low had the spirit of the Crown Prince's V Army sunk after these ten months of battle.

Away on the Somme, the year ended for both sides in an unconquerable morass. 'The transport has to plough its way with horses and wagons through the mud at night in order to take the troops their rations, the guns their ammunition,' wrote Binding. 'Their way is marked by dead horses; many of them fall without being hit, and the mud closes over them. . . . In the morning we crawl back, plastered with mud, horse and rider stiff with cold, our heads sunk on our chests, dog tired and worn out.'

Top right: 'Those of Verdun', a painting by Albert Moreau. Bottom right: French troops move through the mud up to the front. Right: An ambulance column waits behind German lines

du canon de 37 allant prendre position (entre Biaches et la M...
— 1ᵉʳ octobre 19...

Chapter IX
The Price of Glory

Verdun had been saved, but at a terrible cost. Half the houses in the city had been destroyed and nine villages had vanished off the face of the earth. The French had lost 377,231 men, of whom nearly half were dead or missing. 'The German unwisdom in attacking Verdun,' writes Churchill, 'was more than cancelled in French casualties.' The Germans lost at least 337,000.

On the Somme, the British had lost about 420,000 men, the French about 200,000, the Germans probably about 450,000.

In the two battles, the total casualties were therefore more than 1,750,000. The memory of Verdun was to haunt a generation of soldiers — those who survived. The younger officers of 1916 were to be the German and French generals of 1940, deeply influenced on both sides still by the horror they had once lived through. The Somme, fought by the best of Britain's volunteer armies, deprived her of a generation of leaders.

The Verdun salient remained the front line till the very last week of the war, and there were to be further outbreaks of serious fighting. Partly for this reason it retained its full attribute of suffering and horror. The Somme battlefield, on the other hand, became lost in the limbo of the British rear areas when the two new brooms, Hindenburg and Ludendorff, decided to shorten and strengthen the German line by eliminating the Noyon bulge in the middle of March 1917. The German defences were redrawn further back along a straight, strongly fortified line. They called it the Siegfried Line: the Allies knew it as the Hindenburg Line.

This daring and clear-sighted move of Ludendorff's — so much at variance with the rigid ideas held on both sides until now — seemed to make a mockery of the great Somme battle just passed, to set the deadly, week-long struggles for copses and ridges at nothing, to give the Allied victory, costly as it had been in any case, an added hollowness. But the attrition had taken its toll: it had

Left: 'The Price of Glory' a painting by C. Nevinson which savagely reflects the growing feeling of bitterness on both sides

115

been tragic for the British, but desperate for the Germans, who had been very near to the exhaustion Haig was always counting on. Verdun and the Somme had made the saving of ten German divisions, which the new line made possible, a matter of importance.

The Somme battlefield now became just 'the old front', which Masefield wrote of. 'Centre Way, Peel Trench, Munster Alley, and these other paths of glory will be deep under the corn, and gleaners will sing at Dead Mule Corner.'

The Somme, and the successes of the German U-boats, brought to a head dissatisfaction in Britain with the management of the war. Asquith was manoeuvred out of office in December 1916, Lloyd George took his place.

However competent, energetic, and inspiring Lloyd George was to be in running the country in war-time, it was still Haig, protected at home by Robertson, who ran the British war on the Western Front. Lloyd George felt most strongly about the losses on the Somme and Haig's responsibility for them, but could not replace him without estranging much of his own political support. It was a measure of his dilemma that he should go to such discreditable lengths in February 1917 to place Haig under the orders of the new French commander-in-chief. In the end it merely meant that Lloyd George and Haig conducted the rest of the war on terms of undisguised hostility.

The French commander-in-chief was no longer Papa Joffre. Criticism of his strategy of attrition had grown steadily with French anxiety over Verdun, and now the Somme, and in December 1916 he was elevated out of his command into virtual retirement as a Marshal of France. It was Nivelle, taking all the credit for the final counter-strokes at Verdun, who was chosen to succeed him. De Castelnau, Foch, and Pétain were passed over.

Nivelle made a great impression on Lloyd George, as well as on so many others, with his articulate confidence, his show of knowing all the answers, his excellent English: he seemed indeed the man to control the obstinate Haig. But Lloyd George had entrusted the command to a bubble. Briand's government, on whose support Nivelle rested, fell in March 1917; and in April and May, Nivelle led the French army to disaster and mutiny on the Chemin des Dames ridge above the Aisne.

Already at Verdun in December 1916 a French division had gone up to the front bleating like sheep. This was one of several signs, despite the successes, that the French troops could not be driven farther. 'They will not be able to make us do it again another day; that would be to misconstrue the price of our effort,' wrote Lieutenant Jubert, killed at Verdun. 'They will have to resort to those who have not lived out these days.' Verdun, with

its prolonged and personal horror, carried in itself the seeds of the French army mutinies of May and June 1917, when fifty-four divisions – half the army – were affected, and only Pétain saved it from collapse.

Germany had already changed her military leadership in August 1916 with the appointment of Hindenburg and Ludendorff. The country was suffering not only from the losses at Verdun and on the Somme but from hunger. The harvest of 1916 had been disastrous, manpower had been milked from the land, and the Allied blockade was starting to tell in such vital matters as fertilisers. The winter of 1916-17 in Germany came to be remembered as the 'turnip winter'. These difficulties produced conflicting proposals towards the end of 1916 for two extreme policies: the German naval staff urged the declaration, long delayed, of unrestricted submarine warfare; whereas the Kaiser and the Chancellor, Bethmann Hollweg, demanded that peace proposals should be sent out through the neutral United States to the Allies. The latter policy prevailed at first; but when the Central Powers' proposals were submitted on 12th December, even with their harsh basic terms unrevealed, the Allies, under the influence of the uncompromising Lloyd George and the glamorous promises of Nivelle, turned them down scornfully, and the German naval staff was able to have its way, steering Germany onto a disastrous collision course with the USA.

Seeds of despair and revolt

The spirit of the German army was never the same after 1916. Verdun and the Somme had bitten into its soul, though its collapse was delayed till November 1918. The History of the German XXVII Division, which had defended Guillemont in August, says: 'In the Somme fighting of 1916 there was a spirit of heroism which was never again found in the division . . . the men in 1918 had not the temper, the hard bitterness and spirit of sacrifice of their predecessors.'

By the autumn, Brusilov's magnificently game offensive on the Eastern Front in the summer of 1916, which had given the defenders of Verdun that crucial breathing space, had captured over 400,000 prisoners and more than 500 guns. It meant the end of the Austro-Hungarian army as a positive force: the Germans had to fight their battles for them from now on. But to the Russian army too the offensive had been an enormous strain; and when its energy was spent, the economic and political difficulties inside Russia started assuming grave proportions. It was

Left: A working party sets out. After all the suffering of the Somme, the British were able to walk into the old trenches as the Germans pulled back to the new Siegfried Line in March 1917

in this very month, October 1916, that the first riots occurred in Petrograd. The mounting stages of the Russian Revolution were not far off.

Here then, in the great battles of 1916, were the seeds of mutiny, revolution, and despair. It was not just the cost in lives, waste, and mutilation which were to lead to these bigger tragedies, but the belief that the price paid at Verdun and on the Somme had been for nothing. The military deadlock was unbroken. The trench line across France and Flanders held, even if Ludendorff was making a voluntary adjustment. There was no prospect of anything on the Western Front in 1917 other than further head-on assaults; and this was indeed to be the sequence, at Arras, on the Chemin des Dames, at Ypres and Passchendaele, even at revolutionary Cambrai.

In the hope of breaking the trench deadlock, new weapons had been introduced since 1914. The Germans had first used gas at Second Ypres in 1915, and the Allies had steadily retaliated; and phosgene had been tried in the final stages of Verdun. Gas had caused death, disability, and much discomfort; but after the first surprise, its use would never be decisive. With trench-mortars the Germans had a start: 'we have nothing to equal the German sausage mortar-bomb,' wrote Graves in his diary in May 1915. Soon the British had evolved the handy and effective Stokes mortar. Trench-mortars would always be a trial and a menace and drive the troops deeper into shelters; but they could not destroy a trench system. Flame-throwers had been a terrifying weapon of assault at Verdun, until it was realised what fine targets their crew made at a distance. Underground fortifications seemed a paradise of safety to the Germans on the Somme, until the entrances were blown in by artillery and the men entombed. The creeping artillery barrage, as it slowly became perfected, seemed to be a means of protecting attacking infantry right through the enemy lines: the Germans were to outwit it on the Chemin des Dames by a feint withdrawal.

Two weapons appeared in 1916 whose effects were to be felt more in the Second World War than in the First. One was the use of massed aeroplanes. The Germans in February 1916 had succeeded in denying reconnaissance to the French at Verdun by a mass of patrolling aircraft. The French broke the stranglehold by throwing in all their machines as a group. Boelcke's 'Flying Circus' was the counter-development, but caution at the top prevented it

Left: *A column of German prisoners moves back into captivity. Although Germany was on the defensive at the Somme, the attacks there, coupled with the attrition at Verdun in which she suffered as much as the French, had taxed her strength to the uttermost, and her people and army were seriously exhausted*

becoming effective over Verdun. Over the Somme, Boelcke successfully developed co-ordinated fighter tactics against the powerful Royal Flying Corps, and in one month his squadrons shot down 123 Allied aircraft for the loss of twenty-seven. Nevertheless, the British were still strong enough to enjoy the very considerable advantages of aerial observation for their artillery. The aeroplane had to wait many years before more powerful engines gave it the speed and strength needed for truly offensive operations.

The tank was the most important development of the First World War. From its very first use on the Somme on 15th September 1916, untried and unassimilated though it was, the tank gave indications that it could do what it was meant to do — break through the enemy trench line. Its failure then and in the early battles of 1917 lay in its ill-considered use. Those who had nursed it from infancy saw the tank as a weapon in its own right, as a new arm, to be employed as a massed force with its own tactics. Instead, because the numbers, the reliability and the experience were not yet there, the tanks on the Somme were used and thrown away in penny packets. Haig seized on the new tank as just another weapon to help the infantry soldier. The British High Command at this time showed as little understanding of the true purpose of the tank in battle as the French High Command in 1940.

But one of the most misused weapons of 1915 and 1916 was also one of the oldest — the weapon of surprise. Sometimes it was used and at once thrown away, sometimes it was thrown away first. Haig achieved surprise at Neuve Chapelle, but the generals had not the experience, nor the imagination, to follow it up. The Germans achieved surprise with gas at Second Ypres, but were quite unprepared to fill the gap they had created. At Verdun again the Germans achieved surprise with the sheer size of their opening bombardment, but then sent their troops in with elaborate caution; similarly, in June, they failed to capitalise on the shock of the first phosgene attack. On the first day of the Somme, the French achieved surprise, but they and the British were unwilling to move in the forces to exploit it. Rawlinson achieved surprise on 14th July by his night attack, and his corps commanders lost it for him with their dilatoriness. Four tanks achieved surprise at Flers, but the tactics to follow up their successful breakthrough had not been considered.

The very implacability of the Western Front had destroyed strategy. By the end of 1916 any thought of circumventing the trench barrier paled before the terrible size and slaughter of the battles themselves, which seemed to demand a final decision on the Western Front

alone. The immensity and frightfulness of Verdun and the Somme stultified tactics too, until numbers of infantry to fill the gaps left by the dead came to be all that counted.

Too much had been asked of the fighting man. The Russian army and the Austrians were finished, the French army on the verge of mutiny, the German army past its peak, much of it exhausted. The British army still had numbers coming in, but it was to fight the battles of 1917 with reluctant conscripts: the Somme had eaten up the volunteers, the cream of Britain's manhood. The deadlock was so complete, exhaustion on both sides so widespread, that a new access of vitality from outside would be needed to tip the balance. The Americans, driven into the war by Germany's ruthless miscalculations, would be the ones to provide this freshness and strength.

Prince Max of Baden, later to be Germany's Chancellor in defeat, writes of 1916 ending 'in bitter disillusionment all round. We and our enemies had shed our best blood in streams, and neither we nor they had come one step nearer to victory.'

Left: *Two cartoons by Louis Raemakers which sum up the feeling of desperation which had completely replaced the widespread popular enthusiasm of the first two years of the war. 'We must have a higher pile in order to see Verdun' says the Crown Prince to the Kaiser* **(top)**. *'Verdun, the last throw'* **(bottom)**, *the warlords cast away lives in a gamble with death*

Chronology of Events

1914 **3rd August:** Germany invades Belgium and declares war on France
4th August: Britain and Belgium declare war on Germany
14th August: the Battle of the Frontiers begins; the Germans take Liège on the 16th and occupy Brussels on the 20th. They take Namur on the 25th, Longwy on the 27th, Montmédy and Amiens on the 30th, Soissons on 1st September, Laon on the 2nd, Rheims on the 3rd, and Maubeuge on the 7th
23rd August: the battle of Mons: the French and British fall back to the Marne River after General Smith-Dorrien has fought delaying action at Le Cateau (26th August)
5th-12th September: in the battle of the Marne the German line withdraws west of Verdun and the British and French advance cautiously
September: in the battles of the Aisne (15th-18th September), Picardy (22nd-26th September), and Artois (27th September-10th October) the Allies fail to dislodge the Germans
1st-9th October: the Germans force the evacuation of Antwerp by the Allies

10th October-10th November: in the 'Race for the Sea' the Germans take Ghent, Bruges, Ostend, and Lille, but in the battle of the Yser (18th October-30th November) they are prevented from reaching the Channel ports. They also fail to take Ypres

1915 **16th February-30th March:** the French attack in eastern Champagne after bombarding German positions there
10th-13th March: the British launch an attack near Neuve Chapelle and break through the German line for a short distance
22nd April-25th May: the second battle of Ypres — British troops flee as the Germans use poison gas for the first time
9th May-18th June: the second battle of Artois: the French under Pétain break through on a 6-mile front north of Arras and facing Douai
22nd September-6th November: the second battle of Champagne, Joffre's key operation; the French attack on a front between Rheims and the Argonne but the Germans remain firm on the heights between Rheims and Ste Menehould
25th September-15th October: the British use gas for the first time in the third battle of Artois and succeed in driving the Germans back towards Lens and Loos

1916 **21st February:** the battle of Verdun begins; on 25th February the Germans take Fort Douaumont after a heavy bombardment. The French reply with a series of counterattacks but on 2nd June the Germans take Fort Vaux and on the 23rd the fortifications of Thiaumont. Heavy attacks continue until 11th July, with terrible losses on both sides
1st July-18th November: the battle of the Somme, the Allied offensive, now relies largely on British forces because of the high French losses at Verdun. The British maintain a long and heavy bombardment and then advance to Bapaume while the French advance to Péronne. British losses on the first day are 60,000 killed
15th September: the British use tanks in battle for the first time without marked success
24th October-18th December: the French counterattack at Verdun, retaking Forts Douaumont and Vaux on 2nd November and making a total advance of 2 miles

Right: Hindenburg and Ludendorff (top). The new year, 1915, appears from a gun-barrel (upper middle). A cavalryman adapts to gas (lower middle). 'The human tank', a British suggestion (bottom). **Centre:** *A German sentry on the Somme (top). Clemenceau at the Somme (middle). German troops advance in 1914 (bottom).* **Far right:** *The legend of Verdun, a French poster of 1918 (top). 'I had a comrade', a German postcard (bottom)*

Par deux fois j'ai tenu et vaincu sur la *Marne*,
Cyrd, mon frère,
à sournoise offensive de la "paix blanche" va t'assaillir à to...
mme moi, tu dois tenir et vaincre, sois fort et malin.
Méfie-toi de l'hypocrisie boche.

Ich hatt' einen Kameraden

Index of main people, places, and events

125

Author's suggestions for further reading

Blake, Robert (ed)
The Private Papers of Douglas Haig, 1914-19
London 1952
Binding, Rudolf
A Fatalist at War
London 1929
Chapman, Guy
Vain Glory
London 1937
Churchill, WS
The World Crisis, 1911-18
London 1931
Clark, Alan
The Donkeys
London 1961
Falls, Cyril
The First World War
London 1960
Farrar-Hockley, AH
The Somme
London 1964
Graves, Robert
Goodbye to All That
London 1929
Horne, Alistair
The Price of Glory; Verdun 1916
London 1962
Jünger, Ernst
The Storm of Steel
London 1929
Liddell Hart, BH
History of the World War, 1914-18
London 1934
The Tanks
London 1959
Through the Fog of War
London 1938
Palat, Gen BE
La Grande Guerre sur le Front Occidental
Paris 1925
Reichskriegsministerium
Der Weltkrieg, 1914-18
Berlin 1936
Taylor, AJP
The First World War, An Illustrated History
London 1963
Terraine, John
Douglas Haig, The Educated Soldier
London 1963
Thoumin, Richard (ed)
The First World War
London 1963

Acknowledgements:
The author is above all indebted, once again, to Mr Peter Bradley, without whose conscientious assistance — and advice — this book could not have been completed. I also wish to record my gratitude to Messrs Macmillan for permission to reproduce passages from my book 'The Price of Glory, Verdun 1916'.

Alistair Horne served in the RAF and Coldstream Guards from 1943-47. He was a foreign correspondent for the London *Daily Telegraph* and has contributed to *The Times Literary Supplement, The Spectator, Purnell's History of the Second World War* and *Purnell's History of the 20th Century.* His books include: *The Fall of Paris, the Siege and the Commun 1870-71, The Price of Glory, Verdun 1916,* and *To Lose a Battle; France 1940,* which was published in 1969.

JM Roberts, General Editor of the *Macdonald Library of the 20th Century,* is Fellow and Tutor in Modern History at Merton College, Oxford. He is also General Editor of Purnell's *History of the 20th Century* and Joint-Editor of the *English Historical Review,* and author of *Europe 1880-1945* in the Longman's History of Europe. He has been English Editor of the *Larousse Encyclopedia of Modern History,* has reviewed for *The Observer, New Statesman,* and *Spectator,* and given talks on the BBC.

Library of the 20th Century

Publisher: John Selwyn Gummer
Editor: Christopher Falkus
Executive Editor: Jonathan Martin
Editorial Assistant: Jenny Ashby
Designed by: Brian Mayers/ Germano Facetti
Design: Henning Boehlke
Research: Sue Graham

Pictures selected from the following sources: